TRANSFORMED
LIVES

A.R.E. MEMBERSHIP SERIES

TRANSFORMED
LIVES

by Joseph Dunn

ASSOCIATION FOR
RESEARCH AND
ENLIGHTENMENT

A.R.E. Press • Virginia Beach • Virginia

A.R.E. Press
215 67th Street
Virginia Beach, VA 23451-2061

Library of Congress Cataloging-in-Publication Data
Dunn, Joseph, 1937-
    Transformed Lives : by Joseph Dunn.
        p.   cm.—(A.R.E. membership series)
    ISBN 0-87604-413-5
    1. Association for Research and Enlightenment—Biography. I. Dunn, Joseph, 1937-   . II. Series.
BP605.A77T73   1998
299'.93—dc21
[b]   98-37139
                                                               CIP

The *A.R.E. Membership Series*

This book, *Transformed Lives*, is another in a continuing series of books that is published by the Association for Research and Enlightenment, Inc., for individuals who are especially interested in their personal and spiritual growth and transformation.

The A.R.E.® was founded in 1931 as a nonprofit organization to study, research, and disseminate information on ESP, dreams, holistic health, meditation, and life after death. The A.R.E. continues its mission today, nurturing a worldwide membership with conferences, study groups, and a variety of publications—all aimed at helping seekers find paths that will lead to a more fulfilling life, mentally, physically, and spiritually. The hallmark of A.R.E.'s publications is to be helpful and hopeful. A.R.E. is committed to assisting in personal growth and making available nourishing entertainment.

Many of the books published by A.R.E. are available in bookstores throughout the world and all are available directly from the A.R.E.'s mail-order catalogs.

Three new books in this *A.R.E. Membership Series* are sent at no cost each year to individuals who are Sponsoring members or Life members of A.R.E. Each of the titles in this series will become available, in the year after initial publication, for purchase by individuals throughout the world who are interested in individual growth and transformation.

For more information about membership benefits of the nonprofit Association for Research and Enlightenment, Inc., please turn to the last page in this volume.

Contents

Some Thank Yous

Gathering the raw material for this volume became a happy task. It was as though the people who were called on for help spontaneously formed a Study Group and opened *A Search for God, Book I* to lesson one: cooperation.

Jeanette Thomas, the knowledgeable and patient administrator in the Edgar Cayce Foundation, gave much of her time, as well as her knowledge and patience, in directing the inquiry into the invaluable records and the original readings, which are her charge.

Rhonda Miller, who has been recording the stories of changed lives for years in *Venture Inward*, graciously allowed the use of some of her materials, as did Dr. William McGarey, whose magazine columns and books have chronicled the miracles of healing through the application of guidance in the readings. Likewise, Graham McGill allowed the use of some of his reflections on the worth of The Work.

A. Robert Smith, editor of *Venture Inward* since the magazine's birth in 1984, is owed a special appreciation. Under his skilled eye and from his sensitive being, *Venture Inward* has consistently represented a remarkable gathering of evidence, issue upon issue, that the work of the Association of Research and Enlightenment, Inc., is being done, and lives are truly being changed.

The greatest measure of thanks is extended to those individuals who have come to The Work, have applied its guidance in their lives, and have seen fit to celebrate their transformed lives in letters, in stories, in books, and in the spoken word. They are The Work.

INTRODUCTION

Words spoken. Lives changed.

This simply stated cause and effect is the essence of what began in 1901 when a young man lay down and uttered words that were not his own; it is the mission and the passion of what continues today as a worldwide movement.

The spoken words came from a sleeping Edgar Cayce who, for forty-three of his sixty-eight years, entered into a trancelike state and gave readings in response to the sometimes simple, sometimes complex questions put to him.

The changed lives are those of many who came to Cayce and who sought and received answers for themselves and for others as they confronted challenges or sought opportunities.

There are, however, legions more of those who never knew Cayce but who have been touched and changed by the information in the readings, now gathered into a body of material simply called The Work.

It has been fifty-three years since Edgar Cayce, the man, passed on. His life continues to be examined in biographies, both printed and filmed; the information that came through him continues to be analyzed by researchers and reporters; and his very name evokes reactions that range from the respected and serious to the derisive and trivial.

It is The Work that endures quietly, without headline and

fanfare. It is The Work that continues to touch those who discover it and continues to have a life-changing impact on those who make earnest effort to apply in their own lives the guidance that came through the sleeping Cayce.

The information in the readings addresses more than 10,000 subjects. Health, to which the majority of the readings were addressed, reincarnation, dreams, psychic phenomena, and spiritual growth are the broad hallmarks of the knowledge that came through Cayce. Into these fall such modest aid as curing warts and such cosmic guidance as soul growth. Each reading was given for a particular individual who brought into Cayce's small study his or her own quest for answers to a life that was unique.

Through the years, as more and more people have learned of Cayce and the readings, they have applied the advice that came through him for others. And they have found that the advice is sound.

These individuals have come to The Work in myriad ways—through a book loaned to them by a neighbor, from a magazine article in a doctor's office, through a friend who invited them to a Study Group meeting, through camp, a prayer network, a prison, or through a weekend conference held in some near or distant city or town.

What these thousands of individuals have found, since Cayce's passing, are answers to their questions about their life. Those who have listened and truly heard the answers have taken them as their own and they have been changed. They have become the real legacy of The Work. They are the evidence to others, now and in the future, that Edgar Cayce's grand mission in his time on earth—to help others—is being fulfilled.

This volume is a small and random collection of that evidence, a gathering together of stories of a few of the people who have been made better. The stories have been gathered from first-person stories in journals and magazines and newsletters, from file cabinets that house hundreds— if not thousands—of letters that tell of life-changing results from applying principles found in The Work; and from talks with individuals who want to spread the word.

Included also in this collection are occasional excerpts from the readings that seem appropriate as reminders to those who come to these pages that we can find encouragement to pursue our own path to transformation.

What is not reflected in these pages, however, is the commitment and the effort made by those who have benefited from The Work. The late Harmon Bro, who worked with Cayce and became one of his most eloquent advocates, reminds us in his writing that "much of Cayce's counsel was one-shot or few-shot *beginnings* of spiritual guidance."

Change, as the entranced Cayce frequently admonished and as the waking Cayce knew well, is a lifelong process and those whose stories are retold here are in that process: active, working, and—more often than not—joyous.

One cannot help but be moved to prayerful thanks that Edgar Cayce wrestled to defeat his frequent doubts about the value of the gift he was given and became a vessel for The Work that continues to transform lives.

Dear Charles Thomas Cayce:

I just wanted to thank you and everyone at A.R.E. for carrying on with Mr. Cayce's work.

I don't have the money yet to be a sponsoring member, but I'm trying. If I had a job, I would send a gift of $50 or more if I could.

I'm just another seventeen-year-old teenager who's been through a lot of confusion. You have been through it, and so has everyone else. Thanks to you, Edgar Cayce, and the A.R.E., I have found my way back towards my true home with God.

With the blessings of the season and year, thank you and God bless!

Chapter 1

A Skeptic's Graduation: Tom Sugrue

Nineteen-year-old Tom Sugrue, making a last-minute switch in his choice of colleges, found himself in the fall of 1926 surrounded by the majestic mountains of the Blue Ridge on the campus of Washington & Lee University in Lexington, Virginia.

One of the first new acquaintances that this native of Naugatuck, Connecticut, made at the prestigious private institution named for two of Virginia's great heroes was Hugh Lynn Cayce, elder son of Edgar Cayce.

Their first exchange of words was a lighthearted insult about the young Cayce's hometown of Virginia Beach, an insult that he returned in kind. If the meeting wasn't as cordial as one would expect of two college freshmen, each away from home for the first time, it was a harbinger of the difficult, yet deeply devoted, relationship the two would have for most of their lives.

Out of this initially antagonistic introduction between the two would come a path that the popular red-haired student from the North would walk his entire life, guided by information from the Edgar Cayce readings. It was a path that would change Tom Sugrue's life and, as a result of his commitment to The Work, would change the lives of countless others.

The path was a bumpy one at the start. The two college

students argued and, at times, fought. Over small things like their respective hometowns. Over bigger things like their spiritual backgrounds. Sugrue sneered at psychical research and, at least indirectly, at Edgar Cayce's ability. Hugh Lynn found flaws in Sugrue's Roman Catholic beliefs.

The bumps, however, were constructed more of personality traits than philosophical differences. Despite Sugrue's protestations against the psychic realm, he was already very interested in philosophy and religion. Even as a youngster, Sugrue had shied away from his church upbringing, declining to attend Sunday school in a strongly Catholic environment. He spent much of his free time in the town library, looking for answers to philosophical and spiritual questions that would have taxed the minds of many of his elders. He created in his mind his own church, one fashioned after that of the Essenes.

Years later, when he reflected on his hometown environment and its primary religion, he provided a deep insight into his feelings as a young man in that small Connecticut community:

> In two ways they (the people) are different from me. They were resigned to a goal of material success, and they accepted heaven as an advanced state of earthly comfort to be acquired by regular attendance at Mass and the reception of the sacraments. I didn't believe these things, but nobody knew I didn't. I had no idea how I was going to circumvent the business of making a living or the finality and authority of sacramental salvation, but I was going to make a fight of it.

He began that fight by narrowing his choice of colleges to accredited and nonsectarian that offered journalism courses and were located in a setting unlike his hometown. He found that choice in Lexington, and, in meeting Hugh Lynn Cayce, he found much, much more.

Before his first year at Washington & Lee had ended, Hugh Lynn wrote to his father: "I have met one fellow, at least, who will be well known as a writer . . . He wants to get a life reading . . . He is very interested, and I am anxious to get him placed. We get along miserably together, both too sarcastic and disagree on many big ideas, yet must have some attraction somewhere else."

In June 1927, Tom Sugrue went to the sleepy little seaside community of Virginia Beach and received his first reading from Edgar Cayce at the Cayce home on 35th Street.

His life reading painted the portrait of an individual with exceptional mental abilities and "with the love for the delving into those . . . mysteries of every nature, especially as pertaining to thought, mind, or those emanations from same."

The past lives recalled in the reading were near-mirror images of one another in terms of talent:

> [Oliof in England at the time of Alfred the Great]:
> . . . rather the recluse, studying in that of music and chemistry—hating the one, loving the other—setting many of the songs of David to music.
> [A life in the Holy Land at the time of the Crusades]:
> . . . the entity being the teacher and the counsellor to many in that bondage, among those people, and in the urge is seen that innate desire to see the Holy Lands, and *write* of same, and to see same free from any oppression, save those who seek alone to do the highest biddings.
> [Oelom in Egypt at the time of the division of the land and its peoples]: That of the counsel to many for the definite stand for Right as must be taken, and the urge to write that of prose, and of song . . . 849-1

The time that young Sugrue spent with Edgar Cayce and the information in his life reading made a favorable and lasting impression, one that was to deepen through the years for both the man and The Work. Cayce, after the initial meeting with the young man, seemed equally impressed. Only weeks after their first meeting, Edgar Cayce wrote to Sugrue:

Tom, oftentimes one may be so close to a thing that they are not able to see what's going on around them— and while you are, of course, many years younger than I in experience of the things of this life, yet I feel sure— from having met you and being with you a few days— you have been brought up in that environment and have a broad enough view of life, that you are able to be a very good discerner. Now, I realize that we are undertaking a real proposition here. To my mind, it is to be either one of the biggest things that this country has ever seen or it will amount to nothing. I feel sure that— since having contacted the work and the phenomena— you have thought of it considerably, and I would like to ask you—as man to man, as friend to friend—to tell me just what you think of it. Not that I am trying to get you to subscribe to any part or portion of it—for oftentimes our best friends are those who tell us of the faults they see in us or in that we are attempting to foster on the minds of others. So, if you will take the time to do this, I should be more than pleased—and if the skin should be rubbed off 'til it's raw, alright! for I'm sure you have seen the thin places as well as any good that may be behind it all. But, I do not want to fool myself, and I do not want to fool anyone else.

Hoping and trusting you will let us hear from you occasionally, asking to be remembered to your loved ones, and with kindest personal regards from each and everyone here,

I am
Sincerely, Edgar Cayce

Sugrue's response, on August 22, 1927, displayed a remarkable understanding of The Work and his appreciation of it:

My dear Mr. Cayce:
Your letter came as a very enjoyable surprise; I was more than delighted to realize that you had not forgot-

ten me. I have no memory of days more enjoyable than those spent with you at the beach, and the conversations with you constitute moments I treasure beyond price...

It would be untrue to say that I was not skeptical when I came to visit you. It would be equally untrue to say that I was an unbeliever. I have always been attracted to philosophy and theology, my meeting with [Hugh Lynn] and with your work only intensified this interest. I know that when I came to the beach I was willing to be convinced; I wanted to believe. Had I been the greatest of scoffers, the result would have been the same. Frankly, I cannot understand how you, who have seen the great success you have had for an entire generation, can still have room for any doubt or adverse opinion. Like religion, the theory you expound has to shape itself in each one's mind according to his or her ability of conception and credulity. In my case, I found that it was just what I had always believed but hadn't been able to conceive in my own mind. I believe implicitly that you have, and are now about to embark on a larger scale, the greatest humanitarian movement in the country. It is educational as well as physically beneficial; in fact, it is an altogether fitting use for the great power that has been manifested in you. There can be nothing ahead but success, for the Institution is founded on the firm foundation of unselfishness and faith.

Perhaps I am not the one to express an opinion. I am perhaps too "sold" on the thing, too enthusiastic about it, yet I feel that anything of that nature which can so engross and convince one brought up in the most strait-laced of religions, without. I must emphasize, creating any dissention (at least in my mind) between it and the religion I profess, must of necessity be sincere, true, and right.

In the year before us, I can see nothing but success for the Association, its Institution, for you, for your family, and for myself. I am irrevocably wedded to the life of a student, it is my ruling passion, and just now I am sincerely hoping that when next summer rolls around you may be able to find something for me to do at the Institution which will permit me to be there, close to the work and studying it with all the intensity which I can muster.

For the present, I am waiting Hugh Lynn's decision, or should I say yours, or His? In the meantime, I am going ahead with preparations for another year of school, wherever it may be, and spending my idle moments in reading, dancing, and keeping young.

I will not wish you luck, merely your just due, which should be sufficient for the greatest of success. Remember me to Mrs. Cayce, whom I remember so well, and to Edgar, Hugh Lynn, and Gladys. I shall be looking forward to hearing from you, and to meeting you all again, in the not too distant future, let us hope.

Sincerely,
Tom Sugrue

It was the first exchange of letters that would become a lifetime correspondence between the two, often relating to each other the happenings of family and friends, but always focusing on the work that Cayce had undertaken.

Seven months after he had received his life reading, on December 19, 1927, Sugrue wrote from Washington & Lee to Cayce for a physical reading:

I have been in ill health for some time ... I am forced to remain here until school is out because of taking all my cuts while in the hospital ... The doctor seems unable to locate the seat of my trouble and it isn't getting better ... I am desperately in need of a cure and relief, and if you have time, can you give me a physical reading during the holidays?

Sugrue's condition, undiagnosed by doctors during his lifetime, would wax and wane through the years. It was the source of sixty-seven readings that he followed with commitment. Cayce's initial reading pinpointed the genitive (the sex organs) system, where "conditions are the cause of disturbances in the system." The reading recommended dietary changes and periodic cleansing of the genitive system, moderate physical activity, the absence of worry, and above all this: "By following the clean living, *physically, mentally,* and the application of self to introspectiveness as to the application of the body physically and mentally, will keep the body in that way of building towards the application of self in the physical, the mental, and the spiritual forces of the body. Remembering that each are a unit, yet the combination is manifested in the body known as [Tom Sugrue], and that as seen by others is the reflection of the application of the whole as to self and others. Keeping self pure and unspotted from the world. Not as men count that as of yore, but even as the Master gave—being in the world yet not *of* the world, save as the applying of self to the world in a whole . . . " 849-2

Sugrue took the reading to heart, and he also embraced the work that Edgar Cayce was about. He continued to correspond and returned to Virginia Beach in the summer of 1928, spending hours studying and interpreting the readings that Cayce gave for others, keeping notes of his observations of the man and The Work.

While still at Washington & Lee, Sugrue began writing for the Association of National Investigators, the predecessor organization of the A.R.E. He contributed articles for *New Tomorrow* and compiled the annual review of the organization. In August 1929, he requested a life reading for Mary Ganey, a college student he had met in 1926 and for whom his feelings were deepening. The reading offered some cautionary advice, guidance that would later aid him in understanding a sometimes difficult relationship.

All the while, as his physical condition weakened, then improved, then weakened again, Sugrue sought advice through the readings, applying the remedies and following the recommendations.

The bond between Tom Sugrue, the Cayce family, and
The Work was inseparably forged by the time he graduated
in 1930 from Washington & Lee. He came to Virginia Beach
to write for the Cayce organization, but by the fall of that
year the Great Depression and personality difficulties
among some of the Cayce Hospital backers had altered
plans; and Sugrue, who was to also create promotional
materials for the hospital, was without a job.

In April 1931, only four years after Sugrue had first extended his hand to greet Edgar Cayce and within weeks of
the closing of the Cayce Hospital, the novice writer from
Naugatuck revealed in a letter to Cayce the depth of his
commitment to The Work and the impact that Edgar
Cayce's endeavors had made upon his life:

> *If I can possibly get together some little money, I will
> be at the meeting in June. I have promised Mary to at-
> tend her graduation the first week in June and will
> make every effort to do so. Then, if there is reasonable
> assurance that the work will begin after the meeting
> and I shall be accorded a place, I can come to the beach
> and be ready to start. Believe me, nothing would better
> please me.*
>
> *I want you to know how fully in accord with you I
> am, how eager I am to begin work—for me there is no
> other profession in the slightest way attractive or desir-
> able. And I want you to know that I shall have a more
> mature, determined, faithful, and idealistic attitude
> than heretofore. I trust this time our tribulations in the
> past will find a justification in triumph—and because
> we have been through them, we shall be the more wor-
> thy and capable of success.*
>
> *You yourself have known suffering such as few of us
> are called upon to endure. It is from you I take the
> example and the inspiration. All the people of the
> world—except my friends—may ridicule my work and
> deprecate my writings, but so sure as the sun rises I
> shall someday reach the very pinnacle of that fame—*

and it will be as the teacher through such songs and stories as I may spin from the gift God has given me. In your service, working side by side with you in the Christian work of bringing to people the truth we are sure of—I shall be tempered further and to the utmost— and from the womb of suffering shall come that great joy and peace which is so far beyond all earthly raptures.

Despite his efforts to return to Virginia Beach and begin work for the newly formed Association for Research and Enlightenment, Inc., Tom Sugrue was thwarted. With no immediate prospects to labor for the association, his voluntary columns and reports to his hometown newspaper now chaffing him, and with little or no money coming in from his professional writing efforts, he was forced to look for steady employment.

In August 1931, he took a job as reporter for the *New York Herald Tribune* and slowly began to carve out a reputation as a writer and reporter. Although not from a reading, it was advice from Edgar Cayce that prompted his move to New York. Hugh Lynn recalled years later, "Dad said, 'Tom, you should go to New York and get a job on a newspaper, and if I had your skills I'd go to the *Herald-Tribune.*'"

All the while, Tom frequently requested physical readings, as his condition would flare, then subside; he was a constant correspondent to Edgar Cayce and a thoughtful confidante on behalf of The Work and his place in His universe. In October 1931, he wrote:

I am now of the conviction that all our training and hoping and waiting and praying is not preparation in a physical or intellectual way for the high post of service we wish to occupy, but a training for the choosing by the higher forces. Perhaps it will seem to many of my friends in Connecticut (as they have expressed) that I am being forced through a needless and lengthy term of training and suffering, not to mention the ignominy of working under some unvisionary and hard-boiled man. They consider my abilities deserve more of a break than they are getting. On the other hand, I know myself that I am only on the very outermost rim of that spiritual development which will make me worthy of choice for high place—and I shall probably never write anything worthwhile until I attain to the center of the feeling which now and then wells up within me and gives me the conviction that I am on the right path.

I may have things published before long, but I myself contend that I will be thirty-five before I do anything which will deserve the attention of posterity. Meanwhile, it is not half so hard to go along without recognition or reward—as it used to be—and to the eternal glory of your own friendship and work (whatever else may be said about you and about it).

I have discovered myself, my God, and my place in His plan.

One of the items published beneath Sugrue's name the following month was the *Herald-Tribune* story of Cayce's arrest in Manhattan for fortune-telling. The charge was dismissed, and Tom sent Edgar clippings from the *Daily News*, the *American*, the *Times*, and his own *Herald-Tribune*. Along with the clippings was a letter that reaffirmed Tom's commitment to The Work that had become a part of his life: "I've never been happier than when the judge made his decision. I consider it a great personal triumph for you and another for The Work and the people—like myself— who believe in it and intend to see it perpetuated and disseminated amongst the peoples."

The end of the trial was the beginning of Tom's ascent of a literary mountain. His reporting began to attract the attention of editors of other publications. But there was one assignment that Sugrue had given to himself; it was first mentioned in a letter to Edgar Cayce in early 1932. It was to write the story of Edgar Cayce.

There were detours, however, of physical disability and

other literary accomplishments before that assignment would be completed.

For nearly a year beginning in the autumn of 1932, Sugrue would seek readings on increasing pain and disability in his legs, so serious that he was forced to use canes to get around. His mind and his pen were unaffected, though, and he wrote pieces for the *New Yorker* and embarked on an around-the-world trip for a series of articles for *The American Magazine*, which made him a member of the editorial staff in 1935.

He sought a reading that September "on the idea of marrying a certain Miss Ganey, his longtime sweetheart, toward the end of October." There were more cautions in the reading; cautions that would not prevent, but did explain, why the relationship would not always be smooth.

In addition to a book, varied writing projects were now under way with *Scribner's, Tomorrow,* and *Good Housekeeping*. Family changes were also under way. Now married to Mary, Tom and his wife moved in September 1937 from Manhattan to Oceanside, Long Island, in preparation for the arrival of their daughter, for whom Tom requested a life reading shortly after her birth.

But he also needed a physical. Shortly after his wife and child came home from the hospital, Tom himself was admitted to one. An illness that began in his knee was to take hold and refuse its release. The hospital stay and successive treatments in a cabinet under extremely high temperatures reduced the use of his arms and legs and left him sicker and weaker than before the hospital treatments.

He followed Edgar Cayce's advice and moved the family to Clearwater Beach, Florida, where he could undergo near-constant therapy in the warm waters of the Gulf. His father-in-law, however, developed a brain tumor, and the demands of two ill individuals in the family became too much for Mary. Tom, now wheelchair-bound, moved to the Cayce home at Virginia Beach in the summer of 1939. He immediately benefited from the care and affection of his long-ago college roommate, Hugh Lynn, and the rest of the

Cayce family and friends and from advice in the readings that forestalled further physical difficulty.

For the next two years, from June 1939 until October 1941, Sugrue resumed work on Edgar Cayce's biography, work that he had started by making notes and observations when he first met Edgar Cayce.

In the fall of 1941, Sugrue returned to Florida, and a year later *There Is a River: The Story of Edgar Cayce* was published in a limited edition. It was followed by a trade edition in 1943, and in 1945 a revised edition of the book was issued.

By 1946, Sugrue had recovered sufficiently, although confined permanently to a wheelchair, to return to New York. His work proliferated—an autobiography, biographies, magazine articles, a radio talk show—and he traveled the country and the world in pursuit of subjects.

Sugrue received his last letter, this one hand-written, from Edgar Cayce in September 1944, just four months before Cayce passed on. The letter read in part, "I am not doing too well; sort of a stroke I guess. They have come in a kind of series. I hope to get back to work for a while yet, and I want to hold out until the boys get home. I can't much more than put on and take off my clothes. I can't tie my shoe laces or knot my tie. But I am hoping to be better soon. There is so much to be done and so many who need help."

In 1952 Sugrue was admitted to the New York Hospital for Joint Diseases to undergo surgery on one hip. It was a prelude to his vision that he would one day walk again. Complications set in, however, and Tom Sugrue died on January 6, 1953.

There Is a River did not draw much critical acclaim when it was published. Of the ten reviews listed in *The Book Review Digest*, only one was favorable. Of the remaining nine, two were favorable with reservations, and seven were noncommittal.

But, like a pebble tossed into a pond, the book began to send ripples across the country, leading people in need to The Work that had been left by Edgar Cayce. Those ripples continue today to lap the shores throughout the world, attracting individuals.

It seems fitting that Tom Sugrue, the red-haired student wearing a freshman beanie and strumming a ukulele who caught Hugh Lynn Cayce's eye on a Virginia campus in 1926, should carry the message to the masses.

For he, throughout his adult life, was touched by the man Cayce and transformed in many ways by The Work.

His life and efforts were guided, as much as any advice that came through Cayce, by this portion of a reading given for him:

Keep, then, the faith thou hast had in Him; for He is thy strength, He is thy bulwark, He is thy Elder Brother. To Him, *in* Him, ye may find that which will bring to thee alone—joy, peace, happiness, and that which makes me not afraid. For He *is* peace; not as men count peace, not as men count happiness, but in that harmonious manner in which life, the expression of the Father in the earth, *is One*—even as He is *One.*

Keep the faith. 849-11

Chapter 2

OPEN MIND, OPEN HEART: MARGUERITTE BRO

World War II had begun and there were few places in the nation that could boast as many military uniforms as Norfolk, Virginia, and its surrounding communities.

A young sailor stepped up to the woman who had disembarked from a bus and offered to carry her luggage. It was March 1943, and Margueritte Harmon Bro, a missionary-minister of the Disciples of Christ Church and a writer, had just arrived from Chicago at 17th Street and Pacific Avenue in Virginia Beach, Virginia. She was on her way to the Essex House, a modest hostelry several blocks away, to rest before a meeting the next morning with Edgar Cayce. No one was waiting to meet her at the bus station so she let the young serviceman carry her baggage to the hotel.

Bro had come to the Beach as the result of an assignment for *The Christian Century*, a church publication. W. E. Garrison, the literary editor of the *Century* and professor of church history at the University of Chicago, had asked her to review the newly released biography of Edgar Cayce, *There Is a River*, by Tom Sugrue.

In a meeting to discuss the assignment, the founder and editor of the *Century*, Charles Clayton Morrison, indicated by his reluctant approval that the review of such a book was not the normal kind of editorial content that he sought for his magazine. A fourth participant, Edward Schribner

14

Ames, chair of the philosophy department at the University of Chicago and pastor of the University Disciples Church of which the three men were members, observed that the price of an open mind came high.

Bro had accepted the assignment, but only with the understanding that she would pay Cayce a visit before she wrote the review. She wanted to insure that neither she nor her publication were taken in by a hoax.

After her arrival at the Essex House, Bro met with Mr. Cayce even sooner than scheduled. Gladys Davis, Mr. Cayce's secretary, came for her after dinner. Armed with small flashlights because of the wartime blackout, the two wended their way three blocks across some muddy terrain to arrive at the Cayce home in time for the weekly Bible study class.

Bro was treated to Cayce's discussion of two Bible chapters, some light refreshments, and some serious conversation from several of the class members who related that their lives had been changed since they had begun studying with Mr. Cayce. When asked how, they responded that the changes occurred, they felt, because Mr. Cayce "expected the gifts of the Holy Spirit to be as available today as in the time of Jesus and the responsibility of followers to be as forthright."

The journalist's meeting with Cayce the next morning was for the purpose of questioning him on the claims of clairvoyance and the like, but much of the morning was spent in discussing foreign missions and Cayce's devotion to his original church home, the Disciples of Christ, which he had joined when he was twelve years old.

Either persuaded by his conversation that he was no hoax or deciding to give him a personal test, on March 31, Bro joined Cayce's Association and requested a physical reading. The reading found that she suffered from an imbalance between the cerebrospinal and sympathetic nervous systems and that she had a tendency for undue lymph accumulation. The reading recommended osteopathic treatments, use of the violet ray, and doses of pure beet juice.

After the session Margueritte Bro told Gladys Davis, who had transcribed the reading, that she was suffering from arthritis and six years earlier had spent time in clinics in Baltimore and at the University of Chicago, where doctors told her that she would eventually be confined to a wheelchair. She was optimistic after the reading and felt certain that she could get her osteopath's cooperation in the prescribed treatments.

Bro returned to Chicago to write much more than a review of Tom Sugrue's book. Her first note to Edgar Cayce, written immediately after her return, was an indication of the impact that the man and the reading had made on her: "It seems silly to try to say thank you to you all in a few hasty lines. It couldn't be done with a ream of paper. I'm so grateful to everyone, and especially to you personally—and to the leading which brought me to you."

In a matter of weeks she had referred four of her friends to Cayce. One was the president of an organization comprised of the presidents of 1,600 women's clubs throughout the country. Another was the co-owner of one of the nation's leading drug companies.

Of her own reading, she wrote to one of her close friends:

I was glad to have your letter and to know that you are to have a physical reading. When I had mine, I did not know a thing about the procedure, other than Mr. Sugrue's book indicates, and I was amazed at the sort of going-over Mr. Cayce gave me—in his sleep. I still cannot believe the results but he put his finger on a trouble of thirty years and when I followed his simple directions, the thing cleared completely. Sometimes his directions are rather involved and meticulous—as any course of treatment for a stubborn disease is likely to be—but I have seen some amazing results, which makes me keenly hopeful for you.

The results that Bro had seen prompted her to request a life reading in May, as well as to inquire about attending the annual meeting of Congress, the gathering of A.R.E. members. She had become an apostle of The Work.

Bro's review of *There Is a River*—the only favorable one of the time—appeared in the June 1943 *Christian Century*. She explained to the publication's readers that she had gone to see Cayce because she was "so alarmed at the notion of signing her name to a serious review of a great hoax—and at the same time so dismayed at explaining away a phenomenon which could not be explained." The review created little excitement outside the readership of the publication, but the *Century's* editor did receive considerable mail, some of it uncomplimentary. The reaction brought forth an observation from the religion editor for *Harper's*, Eugene Exman, that was remarkable in its insightfulness about Edgar Cayce and The Work: "We have only a kindergartner's understanding of Mr. Cayce's reach of mind, and I don't think he could sustain these gifts if he wasn't focused on the needs of the world."

Margueritte Bro had begun work on an article about Cayce and "these gifts" shortly after she had returned from her first visit to Virginia Beach. In July 1943, she reported in a letter to Cayce that her article had gone off to *Coronet* magazine and they liked it. The story appeared the following month, and the magazine was a sellout the day it was put on the stands.

Almost immediately thereafter, the Cayce home was flooded with written and personal requests for readings, many of them inquiring about family members and friends who were engaged in America's war overseas. Cayce responded. Among those who came to help with the increasing workload was a newly ordained minister who had received the first B.A. in religion given by the University of Chicago. The minister was Harmon Bro, Margueritte Bro's son.

In her first life reading, Margueritte Bro had asked a final question through the sleeping Cayce: "How can I be of use in Mr. Cayce's work?"

She had provided the answer. Unsolicited, unexpected,

and overwhelming in its life-changing impact on thousands, her magazine story about The Work had reached the masses.

Chapter 3

THE EXTRAORDINARY REPORTER: JESS STEARN

Jess Stearn, twenty-eight years old and already a gifted writer and reporter for the *New York Daily News*, walked into a supper club in Manhattan, expecting to meet a friend.

Not finding the person he was to meet, he went upstairs where he was met by a woman he had never seen. Her name was Madam Perez, and she asked him if he wanted a reading.

Stearn, who had gained a solid reputation for his factual reporting and who knew, better than most journalists, how to ferret out the evidence on which to write factual stories, had neither belief nor interest in fortune-tellers.

The woman, not dissuaded, began to tell him that he was a reporter, that his marriage had ended in divorce, that he had two offspring, and that he was giving thought to marrying again.

Because the woman was correct, he listened to what she said about his future. He would, she related, write many books. His third book would be a best-seller and his eighth book would receive acclaim around the world. In addition, she told him that his daughter would become a healer and his son would go into law.

Stearn wasn't persuaded by Madam Perez, at least not at the time. But no reporter closes his or her mind to possibilities. When his third book, *The Sixth Man*, was listed on the *New York Times* best-seller list, at the least he had to remember her predictions. But he remained ever the reporter, looking for evidence.

In 1956, David Kahn, the businessman who had befriended Edgar Cayce and become a supporter of The Work, told Jess about Cayce. The reporter became interested, and five years later, in 1961, he went to Virginia Beach to more closely examine Cayce's work.

His visit was preceded by a letter to Hugh Lynn Cayce from Harold Reilly, who had become a mainstay of Cayce's health regimen as well as a health provider to many of New York's rich and famous:

> *My good friend and well-known writer Jess Stearn and his wife are planning to be with us at the Congress. He is very much interested in the work of your father and the A.R.E. I believe that he is interested in gathering material for either a series of articles or a book."*
>
> *P.S. Jess Stearn has been a feature writer on the* Daily News *for many years; also an Associate Editor on* Newsweek. *He is now devoting his full time to writing."*

Stearn's visit to the A.R.E. was revealing to him and produced part of the evidence that led him to become a major instrument for helping people help themselves through The Work.

The reporter continued to weigh the evidence he had uncovered, and several years later he decided to write a book about Edgar Cayce.

On the day that Stearn worked out arrangements for the book with his publisher, he received a call from a medium called Madame Bathsheba. She told him that Edgar Cayce had come to her and told her he was very pleased that Stearn was going to do a book about him. He feels, she related to the reporter, that you should call it *The Sleeping Prophet* and if you include in the book a discussion of earth changes, the health readings, and reincarnation, it will be a best-seller.

She also told Stearn that he would write the book very quickly and have no problems with the writing. "Anytime you feel you're having difficulty, just look up and ask for his help," she advised Jess.

He wrote the book in three weeks. With little advance fanfare for the book, it climbed the best-seller list rapidly and continues today to sell well.

Since his visit to Virginia Beach and his meeting with Hugh Lynn in 1961, Jess Stearn has been a constant friend and a frequent chronicler, in successful book form, of The Work.

After *The Sleeping Prophet*'s success, Stearn turned his considerable talent to the subject of reincarnation. Despite his experience in writing the book about Cayce, he still harbored questions about the concept of reincarnation. Then he met Taylor Caldwell.

Taylor was a world-famous novelist whom Stearn had met when the former's reputation was large and his relatively small. She invited him to a small dinner party, and they became fast friends. They co-authored several books. Her feelings, like her books, were based on her amazing recall of past events and on very little research. She didn't subscribe to the concept of reincarnation but believed that the information for her books had its foundation in family memory down through the ages.

Stearn, however, found a hypnotist, and Caldwell was regressed to those times that her well-known books described. In regression she started to talk about lives she had lived during these periods and spoke in foreign languages she did not know. She even said during her regression that she and Jess had indeed known Christ and had served with him.

Much of what Taylor said was later verified by Stearn as accurate, and another best-seller, *Glory and the Lightning*, was the result.

The evidence didn't persuade Taylor Caldwell of reincarnation, but Jess Stearn, the reporter, took the concept as his own foundation for another book that broadcast the worth of Cayce's work. *Soulmates: Intimates Through Time* contains his interviews with a number of individuals who received life readings from Cayce and who found their contemporary lives dramatically affected by their past lives.

Stearn's endless energy has resulted in more than thirty books, most occupants of the best-seller list. Two of his recent titles have continued to call attention to The Work: *The Physician Within You,* written in conjunction with Dr. Gladys McGarey, whose holistic approach to medicine derives from Cayce's medical readings, and a forthcoming book on the approaching millennium which focuses on the underlying meaning of Cayce's predictions.

But none of Stearn's books has had greater impact on individuals who are seeking answers—and perhaps on the author himself—than *Edgar Cayce: The Sleeping Prophet.*

Chapter 4

THE LIVES OF THE MANY

Tom Sugrue, Margueritte Bro, and Jess Stearn, as much as any others, brought the work that Edgar Cayce did to public awareness. Scores of books and magazine articles have been written to safeguard that awareness since the last reading was given and since Cayce passed away. But Sugrue, Bro, and Stearn had a firsthand understanding of the pillar upon which The Work was built. They were among the first students, then teachers by example, of the spiritual truth that came through Cayce—the inseparable communion of mind, of body, and of spirit, *always of spirit,* and the Oneness that is the collective Creator, by whatever name and in whatever place.

Perhaps it is because each of them was on a personal quest to better understand the nature of life and living—Sugrue seeking to understand the essence of God, Bro wanting to reach out her hand in love to others, and Stearn critically examining on behalf of others the benefits that came through Cayce—that the first two found themselves embraced in deep and mutual friendship with Edgar Cayce and all three saw early in The Work its power for good and its service for all.

What these three writers first broadcast to the world remains alive and available. Through the decades the physical form of the readings has kept pace with the times. From the blurred carbon copies of original material turned out of Gladys Davis's typewriter and stored in files and boxes to notebooks and then to microfilm and today to electronic dissemination, the material that came through Cayce waits for those in need.

And those in need continue to come—out of longing, out of pain and frustration, sometimes out of fear, frequently out of curiosity, but almost always out of hope for a better, a different, a grander life.

Some, it must be said, leave disappointed.

But those who are open in heart and in mind, those who are willing to apply themselves, and those who are willing to persevere, stay and work and change. These are the stories of some of those individuals. This is a portion of the continuing story of The Work.

*   *   *

It was a New England spring day in April 1976.

Dottie's husband had been out in the small town of Billerica, Massachusetts, a community just south of Lowell in the middle of a landscape dotted with the museums and historical sites of the Revolutionary War, and not far from Thoreau's Walden Pond.

When he returned home that day to Dottie and their four children, ages six, seven, eight, and nine, he carried with him a copy of the book *There Is a River*. It wasn't something that Dottie had requested, but it was something that she discovered she needed. Between its covers was information that would lead Dottie to a new and a different life.

She had been raised a Catholic but had been away from her church for years. As a child she developed a fear of God and, as a result, a fear of death. "One of my biggest fears," she recalls, "was that if someone close to me died, I wouldn't be able to handle it."

After reading *There Is a River*, Dottie and her husband ordered *A Search for God, Books I and II* and joined a Study Group through an ad in the local newspaper.

As a result of what the two of them found between the covers of the books, she began reading the Bible. She hadn't known much about Jesus, but her renewed interest in the Bible stimulated her interest in Him. She wrote to the A.R.E. for the circulating file *Jesus the Pattern,* and she and her husband discussed what they were learning.

As Dottie's understanding of the Master deepened, she made Him her personal Savior, accepting the promises He had made to humankind. She found in her readings a new way to look at dying; holding Jesus as her example, she could accept a peace and harmony in death.

In June, Dottie resigned from her job at Raytheon in order to be with her mother, who was seriously ill with cancer, and her husband, who was making a determined effort to stop drinking. He was unemployed at the time and he needed her to be with him at home as emotional support. He agreed with her decision to leave her job, which proved to be wise.

"It brought about the most beautiful result. I had three months to be with Mom. I was out of work for a year. It was the most beautiful year—the best year—of my life in my sixteen-year marriage. The two of us talked about Cayce and read the Bible. We continued meditating—we had begun shortly after we learned about Cayce—and my husband stopped drinking for that year."

Her new-found faith was tested in August, only four months after she first learned of Cayce. Her mother died of cancer, but Dottie was able to find a beauty in her mother's illness, in how her mother approached it, and how those closest to her mother handled it. "Because of reading the Cayce material, I had an understanding of her death. Sometimes, as the Cayce material says, death is the cure."

In the years after her mother's death, Dottie became a part of the community—serving as a school volunteer, an assistant Brownie Scout leader, and a Cub Scout leader.

But another test awaited. Her husband began drinking again, and his behavior became threatening to her and the children. "But I was getting stronger because of the Cayce material and my meditation."

In 1982, Dottie came home to find her husband dead. He had taken his own life. "When I found him, I felt nothing but total peace for him. Because of Cayce's teachings on reincarnation, I felt his act had been an act of soul growth. Out of his selfishness had come an act of unselfishness in ending the problem he had been causing his family."

Dottie had visited the A.R.E. headquarters in 1986 and returned in 1993 to Virginia Beach. Something inside her said, "This would be a nice place to live." Dottie began to feel as though she would move to the Beach. "When I returned home, everything happened so perfectly for a move. My son, who had been living with me after college, moved away, and by November 1995 I was at Virginia Beach . . .

"I had been a paranoid, fearful person earlier in my life. My God was in a box with rules and regulations, which caused my fears. Cayce's work took this God out of the box and made Him all-encompassing. I can't ever put into words the gratitude I feel toward Edgar Cayce's work. It's my life, my whole life, my way of living."

Among the passages in *Jesus the Pattern*, the circulating file that helped change Dottie's attitude and her life, is the following:

So He, as the pattern for each, makes the way clear, the way open that each soul—as it meets the crosses, endures the temptations and overcomes them—may become an heir, *joint* heir with Him to the Crown of Glory; with power temporal, power mental, power spiritual to become the Sons and Daughters of God, as many as are called—and all that fulfill that purpose for which they, as individuals, are called—and carry on in that manner, overcoming, meeting, bearing within themselves. Not in sorrow, not in wailing, but in the *joy* of the Lord. 262-36

Dottie's way of life has uncounted parallels. Every individual is unique, as Cayce said:

> . . . Personality is that seen by others. Individuality is that which shines out from within, separating one from another. Though one may be but a dot, that dot remains ever individual! Though it may be in line with many lines, yet it—the individual entity—the gift from the Creative Energy, that would have emanations to be within self! yet a portion of the whole. The nearer one becomes to that which will give its *individuality*—yet losing itself in the whole—the *more* individuality one attains! 345-2

But each, in some part of his or her being, seeks to return to that original oneness with God:

> (Q) Should the Christ-Consciousness be described as the awareness within each soul, imprinted in pattern on the mind and waiting to be awakened by the will, of the soul's oneness with God?
> (A) Correct. That's the idea exactly! 5749-14

* * *

Just as Dottie began her journey with the chance encounter with *There Is a River*, others have begun at the same starting point.

Roger was in his early sixties when he faced a terrifying crisis. His employer, an internationally known company, dismissed him, citing poor performance. In one quick executive decision, he lost his pension, medical insurance, and a six-figure life insurance policy that was his ultimate protection for his wife.

In a instant, Roger's pride in himself and in his abilities disappeared along with his job. Despite comfort from his wife, he felt alone. Put into an orphanage at age two, he had no help or guidance as he grew up.

"I was on my own, unable to ask for help or to pray. I didn't know how, or what to pray for."

Shortly after the firing, he stood in the unemployment line, dressed in a business suit, believing that his experience and his background would result in another job. It didn't. He was told that his age and his background would work against him.

"It was the darkest hour of my life. As one of more than five million displaced workers in the country, feeling the deepest depression and despair I had ever known, I began to relate to the homeless sleeping in parks and bus terminals and to people who committed murder and suicide after being fired."

There were positive entries on his ledger, but Roger couldn't see them at the time. Their home was paid for, he and his wife had savings, and they had no debts. He had suffered one heart attack in the past, but was now in good health except for hypertension and had the comfort of knowing that his wife would at least have shelter if something happened to him.

The monthly unemployment check that started arriving was less than the previous weekly paycheck, and Roger and his wife reduced their expenses to get by.

There was another bright side, which also wasn't obvious at first. Roger, an alcoholic with forty years in Alcoholics Anonymous, had developed enormous inner strength. "I didn't recognize that key as God's golden key, the one buried so deeply within the heart of man he'd never think to look for it there. This is the key that unlocks other doors when one is closed."

That strength helped for a short while, but his doubts grew. How could God's plan allow anyone to suffer as he was suffering? He became angry.

Reading the newspaper one Sunday morning, Roger began convulsing and sobbing uncontrollably. He tried to quiet himself so as not to wake his wife. Then it was over. "Little did I know it was the Alpha point for me, a physical catharsis, a purging, a cleansing. I would learn later that it was the spark that triggered the awareness necessary to begin my recovery. It helped me keep my sanity as weeks of job hunting turned into months."

Three months after he had lost his job, he wandered into a bookstore, depressed and carrying thoughts of a vengeance that had been building. A copy of *There Is a River* caught his eye. He had never heard of Edgar Cayce. "I devoured it—and new lessons about forgiveness and faith. It kept me busy and gave me a purpose of which I was not yet aware. I became an avid reader. With the money I saved by drinking free coffee at the fast-food chain, I built up a library of more than 100 books."

But Roger remained unemployed. He began to realize that being fired for poor work performance—even though it wasn't true, as his production for the year had been 110 percent and he had exceeded all goals—and being in his sixties made it almost impossible to get meaningful interviews. He read everything he could find on the Age Discrimination in Employment Act. The more he studied, the more determined he became to right the wrong that had been done him. He found added incentive when he thought back to the darkest days for himself and his wife.

"My new studies were both fascinating and mystifying. I was learning to utilize, not analyze. All paths led me back to the greatest of all mystical books—the Bible—and to the greatest of all psychics—Jesus Christ, and to the simplest of all mystical prayers—the "Our Father." Finally it hit me like a bombshell: I'd had this mystical power all along. We end every A.A. meeting by saying the Lord's Prayer.

"Little by little, I began to integrate A.A. principles of faith and forgiveness into what I was learning by studying Cayce and others."

Roger's last unemployment check was accompanied by a phone call offering a temporary job exercising the legal knowledge that he'd used at his former job. It gave him the confidence he needed to take his former employers to court.

He knew such an action was risky. He could lose everything that he and his wife still had. But he felt deeply and strongly that he had been wronged, that the employer had violated all the rules of decency. He also knew such a lawsuit would be difficult. But he persisted, finally locating a lawyer who would take his case.

After the filing there came one point where he almost withdrew his suit. Postponements had put a drain on their savings and increased the stress. In addition, pretrial testimony had made him realize that his past, including his drinking of forty years before, would be brought out in public. But his lawyer advised him to simply tell the truth.

The trial lasted five days. His wife supported him with her presence every day, although the proceedings were difficult for her to observe.

After the jury had been out for five hours, the company offered a six-figure settlement, which Roger and his lawyer accepted.

After the settlement, his former company wanted a requirement that Roger remain silent about the entire matter. But he refused and formed the Golden Axe Club, dedicated to helping others fight age discrimination.

"I want others to know they can forge their Golden Axe into a Golden Key, as I did."

The kind of effort Roger made on behalf of others is a touchstone of The Work that he found in the pages of a book that he found in a bookstore:

> . . . For all that ye may ever keep is just what you give away, and that you give away is advice, counsel, manner of life you live yourself. The manner in which you treat your fellow man, your patience, your brotherly love, your kindness, your gentleness. That you give away, that is all that ye may possess in those other realms of consciousness. 5259-1

* * *

The fifth-grade teacher at Willoughby T. Cooke Elementary School, located just a few blocks from Edgar Cayce's home on Arctic Crescent in Virginia Beach, began reading to her class from *There Is a River.*

One student in particular listened carefully. His name was Melven, and that night he slept on his school books, hoping to emulate the young Cayce's ability to memorize his spelling book by sleeping on it. The hoped-for classroom result didn't happen, but the young fifth grader had begun to study a much greater lesson—that of spiritual growth.

After high school, Melven was drafted into the Army and volunteered for duty in Vietnam. "After ten minutes there, I knew it hadn't been a good idea, but I also knew that I would return home."

He did come home and he brought with him a personal connection to Buddhism and a knowing that he had much to learn about his spiritual life.

Once back in the United States, he attended college, majoring in art and minoring in religion. He studied *A Search for God* and whatever else he could locate on the subjects of metaphysics and religion.

Though Melven began a career in commercial art, his heritage—his father was a firefighter—became an inner voice, which he heard clearly, and he soon followed in his father's bootsteps and was saving lives and property from the ravages of fire.

Involved in work that often brings into his life the tragedy of homes destroyed, lost lives, and the pain of being unable to save a child, Melven held to one of the underlying principles of the Cayce work and other metaphysical concepts: Nothing happens by chance.

"There is a reason for everything, even though we may not be privileged to know or understand it at that moment. It doesn't take away the sting, especially when children are involved. But it does help me cope. And it hasn't gotten easier over the years; it's gotten harder."

Melven also helps his colleagues work through their questions of why something so tragic occurs to individuals. "It's amazing how many firefighters are interested in metaphysics. I'm always passing along things like *Autobiography of a Yogi, The Tibetan Book of the Dead*, books on the Fatima prophecy, or the Cayce material."

His association with The Work has brought him a realization that spiritual evolution is represented in many new awakenings, new vistas. "Some people," he said, "want that big experience, but I see it as a process of little things all along the way."

Melven echoes the words that came through Cayce as guidance to a thirty-five-year-old teacher in 1932:

So, in the contacts day by day, in the daily labors, let thy yeas be yea and thy nays be nay, that the *glory* of Him may find that little leaven that leaveneth the whole lump. So will the life, the purpose, the work that thou doest day by day, grow in interest in, interesting, and the approach will be here a little, there a little, line upon line, that *His* glory, His love, is set forth in thine acts day by day. 256-4

*   *   *

Margaret had lost hope for a joyous life after surgery on her hand left her crippled. She had never heard of Edgar Cayce nor did she subscribe to the beliefs and concepts that are at the heart of The Work.

Then she read *There Is a River.* Her inquiring mind wanted to learn more about what she had read, so she joined the A.R.E. and began to study many of the topics that are covered in the readings.

Experiences that could hardly be explained by logic began to occur. During meditation and sometimes late at night, she found herself writing poetry with the hand that normally could not sign her own name. From the words that were written she found answers to many of her questions and learned about God, the universe, and reincarnation, which she had been unable to accept.

Some months after she had begun her writings during meditation, the word *paint* came to her. At first she reacted to the word as if it were a cruel joke, but she eventually did take up a brush and began painting.

"I was using castor oil packs, peanut oil rubs, and many other simple remedies found in the readings, but I truly believe that the mind free of doubt and condemnation, plus a strong desire to be with God, is the real miracle worker."

Her acceptance of reincarnation made her a better Christian and brought her closer to the Creator. She was able to reject the premise that all illness comes from sin.

"If I were to believe that my illness was due to the sins that I had committed in this life, then I would also have to believe that whoever judged me and passed out the sentence was very unfair. In my opinion, God is love. I no longer ask, 'Why me, God?' I may have lost a hand, but I have uncovered hidden talent that might have remained buried if I had not listened to the teacher within."

Margaret's attitude toward the information in the readings coincides with what the readings themselves say: "The information to help the self is in the readings, how we accept and apply it to the self is our part, and the end result might turn out to be the best thing we have done in this lifetime."

*   *   *

The book came as a gift from a friend. Its pages would constitute a road map for her life.

As a teenager, Elyse had questions that received no answers during the times she spent in church. Her young mind was focused on subjects such as the Pyramids and the Book of Revelation.

The gift of *There Is a River* in the mid-1950s began to provide answers to her questions and set her on a course of self-discovery.

Self-study for almost eight years led her to a gathering in

1964 of the A.R.E. prayer healing group in New York City.

"When I went to that first group meeting, I was ready. There was an immediate change. I felt the spiritual energy rising, and I was aware of sound, music, and color in a completely different way."

Those elements were part of the fabric that made up Elyse's life. She was a singer and dancer, and through meetings with other creative individuals involved in the A.R.E. in New York, her artistic sense began to expand. Dreams, meditation, and listening to her inner voice prompted her to write and produce successful musicals, and those activities have played a large role in her personal life.

Her life has been built, stage by stage, "with each milestone coming from what I learned from the Cayce readings."

*   *   *

Al passed his own milestone when he read *There Is a River*, but he had begun many years earlier to understand that there are many sources for guidance in one's life.

Al's first experience came when he was studying engineering in 1949 at Cornell University in upstate New York. He developed trouble in his eyes so serious that he could no longer study. Unable to get immediate help at a clinic, he accepted a friend's offer to take him to a healer near Buffalo.

"She went into a trance state, and her guide began communicating through her. She did a laying on of hands. After she had put her hands over my eyes, the pain and the pressure began to subside. It was enough to get me functioning again and back to my studies."

The healing of his eyes opened Al's mind to the possibilities of guidance beyond the normal. He engaged the healer in questions about numerous topics while she was entranced—not the typical approach for an engineer, but one that met many of his needs.

"It just seemed natural, like an ordinary conversation.

From an intuitive standpoint, I knew what I was hearing was truth. I accepted this as a source of wisdom from which I got a lot of guidance for my life."

Al completed studies for his degree, accepted jobs in the engineering field, and began to explore the realms of the metaphysical for his personal life.

His discovery of *There Is a River* and its story of Cayce and The Work led him to an A.R.E. conference in 1958, the same year he and his wife became members of the Search for God Study Group in Pittsburgh. Two years later, they started a second group in the city, now the second oldest Study Group in the country. Since his introduction to the Cayce work, Al has become one of its most active workers and supporters. He lives much of what the readings recommend for spiritual development, including his focus on the ideal of oneness, the foundation for the spiritual life that is offered to those who apply themselves and the principles that came through Edgar Cayce.

*   *   *

Elsie had been married only a brief time when she was diagnosed with a serious heart condition and given only months to live.

While in the hospital, she ran across a book that recommended an individual become closer to God so that person could heal. Her nurse's training and experience rebelled at the thought of any process having the ability to heal except through the knowledge and treatment based on medical principles.

But Elsie also had years of experience in the power and accuracy of dreams. She had a dream that seemed to suggest she keep an open mind and experiment. Her acceptance of the dream's meaning led her and her husband, Bill, to examine the concept of reincarnation and, as a result, they read *There Is a River*.

When Elsie and Bill finished the book, they called Edgar Cayce and requested readings for each of them. The three quickly formed a bond, and Elsie's reading said that she and Cayce had been friends in four previous lifetimes. She received readings for her physical condition and, by following them, she ceased to have the heart problem.

Elsie accepted Cayce's work as authentic and helpful and felt that she was living proof. She began to talk with him about her dreams and the inner guidance she received in the form of visions and inner voices; until that time she had told only her husband.

Meeting Edgar Cayce and hearing him talk about the importance of dreams gave her the confidence to begin lecturing. She also developed a deep belief in the potential good that could be found in the readings, and she started A.R.E. Study Groups wherever Bill's sales executive job took him. She began a book on the life of Edgar Cayce but shifted her topic when a voice told her to write a book on dreams. The result was *Dreams: Your Magic Mirror* which continues to be taken down from shelves in libraries and book stores and which has, in its own way, introduced individuals to The Work and helped to change their lives.

*   *   *

When Stephen was nine years old, he and his six siblings were orphaned. His mother had left the family a year earlier, and the following year his father died in an automobile accident. The children were sent to a state orphanage, where they were among 500 children who were looked after, schooled, and given a weekly exposure to religious services. When Christmas came, each child was invited to a family's home. Stephen's family introduced him to a midnight service in the Episcopal Church, where the liturgy and the ritual made a deep and favorable impression on him.

He continued to question the reasons that his parents were no longer with him, although his mother, who had left the family for another man, did visit once a year. When he was thirteen, a dream helped the healing process. In the dream, he walked down a hallway and came to a door. He was told he had one hour. When he opened the door, he found his father sitting on the bed. He realized that his father was dead, but he hugged him and talked with him, saying he was mad that his father had died and left him. Then he had to go.

"That dream," he said, "always stayed with me. It was the first time I felt God's intervention. It was very healing for me." It was a prelude to other powerful experiences that awaited him and would transform him.

While shopping in a record store at age sixteen, he found a book on yoga, began thumbing through the pages, and became intrigued with the chapter on karma. "That was the first time God answered the question of why I suffered. It was the first time I felt like I had some personal responsibility for my suffering."

The Sleeping Prophet, purchased two years later in a drugstore, was a major influence on him: "That was a very important book for me. The chapters on karma and reincarnation had a powerful effect and pushed me on my spiritual quest."

But Stephen soon found himself on another, more dangerous quest in the jungles of Vietnam. Enlisting in the Marine Corps, he was sent into combat in 1969. Four months later, he was wounded in the legs and chest by shrapnel, drifting in and out of consciousness. Questions about God and life after death came to him as he lay bleeding on the hillside, but he had the faith that there was a God and that if he died, it would be okay.

Stephen was pulled off the hillside and out of the combat zone, flown to a hospital, and later sent home to face the protests against the war in which he had served and been wounded. Suffering trauma, he turned toward religion, earning a master's degree in theological studies and a master's of divinity at Methodist Theological Seminary in Ohio. That was followed by assignment to his first church, a small congregation in Maine.

From there he entered a different kind of ministry—as a therapist at a veteran's counseling center in Bangor, and then as a leader of a parish offering holistic health services. "I've always been attracted to the spiritual aspect of prayer and healing," he said. "I see Cayce as the father of holistic medicine, and if people have physical problems, I encourage them to check alternatives, including Cayce."

Stephen embraces openness as an ideal, which sums up his self-assessment about transformation. "The major transformation in my life is that I used to have a lot of *shoulds* and *musts*. I'm more patient about differences now. My theology is large enough to include ritual, liturgy, reincarnation, dreams, healing touch. I work with people of all religions and sometimes no belief at all. I see my path as teaching and exploring spiritual ideas. My ideal is to open to others and to God," much as an eighteen-year-old boy once opened himself to the ideas in a book about Edgar Cayce and The Work.

*   *   *

The phone call was devastating.

As Barbara listened, the caller identified himself as a mortician in a distant state. He was calling to seek guidance in the disposition of the body of Barbara's mother, killed in an automobile accident only hours earlier and hundreds of miles away. He had assumed that police had notified Barbara earlier. They hadn't. Her shock yielded quickly to a deep and painful sense of loss. Her mother, her best friend, was suddenly gone.

Questions came, especially the need to know about life after death. The questions went unanswered by friends and by the pastor who was counseling her. She searched her Protestant background for something to cling to, but nothing came. She believed in God, but it was a distant God—a God to be worshiped, obeyed, and feared.

Some weeks later, still in grief, she heard the voice of her mother: "Barby, I'm here. I'm all right. I want you to go to the library and find the book, *There Is A River*, about Edgar Cayce. Read it and believe."

Barbara at first couldn't accept that she had heard her mother's voice. But as she thought more and more about the words, she accepted them, even though she had never heard of Edgar Cayce.

She found *There Is a River* and learned from a family friend that her mother had read the book shortly before her death. She evidently hadn't mentioned it to Barbara because, as Barbara felt, "I was so immersed in myself and my problems that she must have known I wasn't ready, not for something so profound and potentially life-changing. And maybe she wasn't sure of it herself, not until she went through that door called death."

Barbara spent a long time examining the story of Edgar Cayce, moving on to *Many Mansions* and *The Sleeping Prophet*. For a while nothing stuck with her, and she returned to conventional concepts. But she was drawn back to Cayce, and when she returned, she stayed.

Through Study Group she began applying principles and tools for transformation in the quest for spiritual growth. Through meditation, she learned who she was, where she'd been, and where she was going.

Her outlook gradually changed from habitual pessimism to near-habitual optimism. Her physical and emotional health improved. She began to look within instead of to others for encouragement and critique, and she came to know that responsibility for her experiences rested solely with her.

But the greatest gift, she said, "the greatest blessing beyond all blessings was and remains that I could meet a most loving God on His terrain, not 'out there' but *within me*."

Chapter 5

FROM THE FILES: BOOKS

During Cayce's lifetime, especially after publication of Margueritte Bro's article in *Coronet* magazine, the postman brought letters and cards from people seeking help. At times the mail came in bagfuls, requiring extra help to respond to the requests for aid and readings.

Today the letters and the cards still come, unsolicited but always welcome as a sign that The Work lives on. They come from individuals who have found help in applying some suggestion or some principle from the readings in their lives. The letters reside in filing cabinets throughout the organization, tucked away as quiet evidence of the life-changing impact that The Work continues to have when it is welcomed by a person into the never-ending process of transformation.

* * *

My life changed when I read There Is a River. *I knew as truth what I read. I have a very small Cayce library, but it all started my growth as I relearned so much. It has helped me during my twenty-two-year-old son's illness and subsequent death from a carcinoma. Because of what Cayce teaches and my readiness to be open to it, I was able to assist my son in his crossing over. I couldn't have—without the knowledge that Edgar Cayce gave me.*

*   *   *

My introduction to the Cayce material came twenty years ago. At the ripe age of eighteen, my father gave me The Sleeping Prophet *to read during my Christmas break from college. I read it and found it fascinating—the seed was planted (just as I'm sure my father planned it!). After his death, I turned back to the Cayce material to help me get through the grief of his passing. The more I read, the more my father communicated with me from the other side. I was opening up so to speak.*

But the ripples of one man's gesture do not stop there. When two of my close friends' babies died—one at five months and one at six months—I shared with them books and my faith. They have both told me it helped them accept and come to grips with their losses. Through this simple act of sharing, the A.R.E. has acquired another member and three more avidly interested people. And that doesn't count whom they themselves have talked to! Some people do not believe that one person can make a difference—oh, how my father would chuckle at that!

*   *   *

The Sleeping Prophet *opened up all the Cayce material for me . . . the A.R.E. and the Cayce material have changed my life and who I am. I am so blessed by this work, and I try every day to pass that on to someone else in whatever small opportunity I have at hand.*

*   *   *

As an eighteen-year-old in the Army, I heard a discussion in the barracks about Edgar Cayce. I read There Is a River *and thought it was mind-boggling, to say the least. Twenty-three years later, at age forty-one, I was told I had terminal*

*cancer and started looking for answers—life, death, etc.
Again became interested in Cayce material, and it has been
no small part of my complete recovery. That terminal diagnosis was fifteen years ago, and I don't have cancer now, nor
will I in the future.*

* * *

*I'm sure it was not by accident that years ago I came across
the book* The Sleeping Prophet *by Jess Stearn. That was a
very trying time in my life. I was drawn to the book like a
magnet and couldn't put it down once I started reading.
Since then, through the A.R.E. I have learned many things,
especially, as Cayce put it, how to "turn stumbling blocks
into stepping stones." I never knew how to meditate, but
through A.R.E. I have learned how to have true inner peace
through meditation and have shared the same with others
who were going through depression and bad times . . . There
are no words to describe the many blessings I have enjoyed
because of you.*

* * *

*I feel as if I've been cured of the incurable. I was a heroin
addict, alcoholic. I read* The Sleeping Prophet *by Jess Stearn
while sitting in rehab. Since then, a whole new world of pos-
sibility has opened up. I am now a receiver of the once-
thought unreceivable. I love myself and the awareness that
came along with it. May we all continue to listen and hear
God's greatest gift, life.*

* * *

When I read There Is a River *in 1951, it led to my career
choice as a minister. Since then the Cayce readings have in-
spired and sustained me. I can point to no particular remarkable experience, just the overall good health and
positive frame of mind that have resulted. I hope I can repay*

*in part the enormous debt I feel to Edgar Cayce and the
A.R.E.*

*I have always told everyone who asked me "what was the
moment of your greatest change in life—a day which
changed the direction of your life completely?" that it was
the day when I read* There Is a River—*nothing after that was
ever the same for me again. It changed my life totally and
what I did with it. It is even now the greatest life-changing
process in my life, and Cayce's teachings inspire me daily,
help me through every crisis and upheaval in my life, and
the A.R.E. Prayer Services has been a lifeline in times of need.*

* * *

*I got involved with the A.R.E. through my dear friend
whom I met while at Dr. Wigmore's Health Institute in Bos-
ton. It was when I first learned that our dreams have meaning. She suggested my reading* Dreams: Your Magic Mirror
*when I returned home. Sometime later, after returning
home, I was casually speaking with an acquaintance from
school days when the name Edgar Cayce literally stood out
from the page at me. It was as if it were lit up and glowing
with energy. I asked him about helping me find the dream
book. He steered me to* The Sleeping Prophet *and* Many
Mansions.

*Everything has whirlwinded for me since. This opened
doors for me that I never knew existed. A lot of life's questions were answered for me. Life started coming together—
every piece (so to speak) that I picked up was fitting.*

*Little did I know that my pouring out my heart to God for
answers after the death of both of my parents would start
me on my life's purpose. Edgar Cayce materials and books
on him and his works helped me to come to terms with
death and dying, and now I can finally use this life for living
and service to help others. I truly know what it means to be
born again. It is like I just started really being alive. It is
so-o-o-o wonderful. Each day is beautiful. I have never been
so glad to be alive and here at this time in our history.*

* * *

My brother-in-law gave me a copy of There Is a River *in June of 1991. I didn't know it at the time, but finding out about Edgar Cayce and finally accepting the reality of reincarnation at the age of thirty-five was the first step in my healing process. By January 1994, I knew there must be something wrong with me that would cause me to make the many painful life choices I had made. There were some annoying, though not serious, physical maladies. But it was the emotional turmoil that was the most painful. That month I began earnest prayers for healing though I had no idea what needed healing.*

By adopting the concepts set forth in the readings and learning about the Universal Laws, I am nearing the end of my therapy less than a year after starting it. Through hypnotherapy, I was able to see some of the past lives I shared with current family members and how this lifetime came to be.

I will be forever grateful to Mr. Cayce for his commitment to bring healing into the lives of so many people. This gratitude extends to all who have worked so hard to spread the information contained in the readings. It's made a world of difference in my life. It's enabled me to heal from a horrible experience many never recover from. And learning that it is truly God's will for each of us to be whole and healthy and learning how to pray for healing give me hope for the recovery of the rest of my family.

Chapter 6

THE GIFTS OF GROUPS

In the mid-1950s Jim had moved to Dallas, where he was an up-and-coming architectural apprentice.

"I was completely ego-oriented. I had set as my goal to be the best damned architect in Texas. I didn't care whose toes I had to step on."

He was well on his way toward that goal when his involvement in a Search for God Study Group stimulated serious examination of his life and his belief systems.

"I realized I was a Christian in name only. I was not really making any effort to truly become a Christian. I finally began to become honest with myself. Then Hugh Lynn Cayce came to Dallas, and he talked about the importance of ideals, of opening one's self up by setting an ideal in life, and about using prayer and meditation to work toward an ideal."

Several months after Hugh Lynn departed Dallas to sow the seeds of The Work in others cities and towns, Jim set aside time in his office for prayer and meditation. He became aware of his fears and anxieties. Slowly at first, then with more and more certainty, he defined his own ideal: peace.

His calm and compassionate reaction to a terrifying excursion with a knife-wielding kidnapper told him he had come a long way toward that ideal.

Jim was driving home from his Dallas office at the close of another business day when he stopped to offer a nicely dressed young man a ride. The two exchanged the casual conversation that two strangers do for about five miles of travel.

Suddenly, the passenger pulled a switchblade knife and told the driver, "I need your car. You just keep driving where I tell you."

For the next two and a half hours Jim drove the back roads of North Dallas County as his abductor instructed. They talked a little, and Jim was able to learn that his captor and several others needed a car that night for some untoward mission.

Jim's immediate concern was for his wife, waiting at home. He knew she would be worried and asked his abductor if he could call her. His request was refused.

His next concern was for the man holding a knife on him. He began to pray for his passenger, then for himself.

About 8:30 that night, his abductor told him to pull over and get out of the car. He did as he was instructed, and the passenger shifted to the driver's seat and pulled away in the new 1963 Plymouth.

With some help from a passing stranger and the Richardson, Texas, police, Jim was finally able to get home that night.

Immediately, he and his Study Group members held prayer and meditation time for the young man and his accomplices—releasing them and their activities to Spirit.

Jim got his car back, the worse for whatever use it had been put to. The lieutenant on the Richardson police force asked him if he wanted to press charges if any of the carjackers were apprehended. "I told him 'no.' I knew that under karma, they would receive a far more exacting sentence than civil laws impose."

Years later, as Jim reflected on his hours of being held at knife point, he said, "By the time I was forced out of my car and he drove off, I loved that young man."

More importantly for Jim and his life, he had passed an

enormous personal test—he had felt no fear during his ordeal, and he was at peace.

The feeling of peace had come as the result of a lot of introspection, a lot of work with prayer and meditation, and as the result of a constant theme through the Cayce work: "Set an ideal."

Jim and his wife, as Study Group hosts in Dallas and elsewhere for many years, have seen the miracles of prayer and Study Group work in the lives of numerous individuals, including Jim's own life. Today he fosters the establishment and the growth of that movement around the world.

The strength and support that Jim, his wife, and tens of thousands of others have found in A.R.E. Study Groups are the legacy of fourteen men and women who sought help from Edgar Cayce in September 1931.

By that year, Cayce's work had been under way for thirty years. Most of the readings addressed two areas: health and spiritual development. The health readings provided a diagnosis and primarily natural treatments, often obscure but unusually effective, to individuals who came to him with complaints of a wide range of ailments. Life readings gave individuals an understanding of the planetary influences on their lives, their activities for good or ill in past lives, and advice about how to find their mission in life, how to develop spiritually, and, often, how to meet the challenges of relationships with others.

The group of fourteen people in 1931 was engaged in the comparative study of some of the world's great religions, seeking universal truths that would increase their knowledge and understanding. In September they approached Cayce for further guidance. At the time, some of the members of the "study club," as they called themselves, were interested in becoming more psychic; others wanted to become more spiritual; still others wanted to know how to make a contribution to the world. The common thread among all of them was the desire to discover greater meaning in their lives.

Cayce tested the depth of their desire and their sincerity

by telling them that they could make a great contribution to the world only if they were committed to their goal. The fourteen agreed among themselves to work together and to adhere to certain guidelines:

• Each would meditate every morning in his or her own home, realizing that fellow club members were also meditating.

• They would make every effort to apply the guidance that came from the readings, telling the others of the insights that came to them as a result of the application, and being sensitive to the insights and guidance that came to them individually in meditation.

• They would ask Cayce about their individual progress and the group also would seek answers through him about the lessons the group was to learn.

• They would attempt to put into their own lives what was being studied, and they would record their personal experiences for possible incorporation in a text they would write.

• Lastly, they agreed that they as a group would not move forward to the next lesson until each individual in the group had learned, understood, and applied the current lesson.

It is doubtful that any one of the fourteen realized at the outset what his or her commitment would mean. The series of twenty-four lessons that were outlined in the subsequent readings required eleven years to complete, as time is measured. The first twelve lessons became *A Search for God, Book I*. This collection of spiritual principles, first published in 1942, has transformed thousands and thousands of individuals, as lives are measured.

Once the first twelve lessons were published, other groups formed, using mimeographed copies of the book as their guide to a more fulfilling life. The remaining twelve lessons were finally published in 1950. By then, a worldwide movement of A.R.E. Study Groups had evolved, a movement that continues to grow and to offer individuals a path to spiritual growth and to change.

The preface to *A Search for God* concludes with this paragraph:

"There is nothing new here. The search for God is as old as humanity. This book is passed on in the hope that through it, during the trying times ahead, many may glimpse a ray of light; that in other hearts it may awaken a new hope and vision of a better world through application of His laws in daily life."

More often than not, when one introduces *A Search for God* to a group dedicated to a common purpose, what emerges *is* something new in the way of lives transformed into better instruments for good.

A Search for God groups are as varied as the individuals who come to them and are as diverse as the reasons that bring the individuals into this special community of seekers. Groups throughout the world form, sometimes diminish in members and fade, often grow in strength, and welcome new members in as others move away or move on.

There is a constant, however, no matter what the size of the group, its long or short history, its location, or its topic at any given moment. That constant is contained in the title to its handbook: "a search for God, by whatever name He or She is called and in whatever form He or She appears to each of us." Laughter, too, is a constant when people gather in such a united purpose.

*   *   *

The Saratoga, New York, Study Group #1 is an example of a community of souls seeking a closer union with God through shared hopes and dreams, fears and disappointments, and the book that the fourteen original men and women created through their long work with Cayce. The group began meeting in 1974 in the basement of the public library.

Graham McGill, one of the group's original members and a former newspaper journalist, author, and writer of magazine articles, authored an informal word-portrait of the group and its members. That picture, save for a modest change of a characteristic here and a feature there, is a portrait of Study Group activity. Anywhere. In any year:

"The library basement had worn orange carpet, fluorescent lighting, his-and-her restrooms, inadequate heating, a tiny kitchenette, and plastic chairs. We were responsible for setting up the chairs, restacking them afterward, bringing our own refreshments, vacuuming the carpet, turning down the heat, and locking up when we left," Graham recalled.

The group started each meeting with the commitment "to gather our thoughts to our common purpose, which is 'to know ourselves to be ourselves, and yet one with God.'" It is a beginning that has its roots in a reading given in Virginia Beach in May 1943 for a sixty-one-year-old woman: "And it is for that purpose that He came into the earth; that we, as soul-entities, might know ourselves to be ourselves, and yet one with Him; as He, the Master, the Christ, knew Himself to be Himself and yet one with the Father." 3003-1

The group modified the suggestions in *The Handbook for A.R.E. Study Groups* in order to meet the unique needs of its members. They met biweekly rather than weekly; they wanted the off-week as time to be with their families. They started the meeting with an informal period to unwind and get reacquainted rather than with a reading from *A Search for God.* Its normal agenda: a moment of silence, an opening prayer, discipline sharing, reading from *A Search for God,* updating the prayer list, then meditating.

"We took seriously the advice from the readings—'make haste slowly,' so we tended to discuss each sentence of the lesson at great length, so slowly that one member, absent for one meeting, accused us of making haste backward," Graham recalled.

They sought specific answers and guidance from A.R.E. headquarters in the early going, but were counseled that they, as a group, must come to their own conclusions.

The members alternated the leadership role, although there were occasions, as Graham remembers, that scratching one's head or stretching an arm upward for comfort could be interpreted as volunteering. Graham, with a barbershop quartet background, once criticized the group's chanting. As a result, he was unanimously nominated as the chant leader. Despite his leadership, the group managed to frighten off a policeman who had come to check on the darkened basement. Expecting him to switch on the lights, the group held its collective breath before chanting. No lights, so the chanting started, and the policeman beat a hasty retreat without a glance back.

When the group moved into members' homes for meetings, the chanting drove pets up the stairs. When several of the members went camping in the Adirondacks, the chanting silenced surrounding rock music from radios, earlier cursing from neighboring campers, and the rumble from a nearby gas engine.

But leadership is leadership, no matter where the leader is. Visiting across the country in Seattle, Graham received a phone call from the group requesting that he lead the group in their meditation chant via a long-distance phone call. Although self-conscious in front of his relatives, he relented. "Ahhh . . . ray . . . ohhmmm" sounded across the phone lines from West to East.

As Graham pointed out, "There is more to SFG work than fond memories. As the readings hold out, 'Some of you are given to be ministers, some teachers, some healers, some interpreters.' In various ways we've realized this promise, sensed the Presence, heard the Call, felt the touch of the Divine."

Dave, for example, has served as a trainer in psychic development at A.R.E. conferences. He expanded the minds of his high school students with insights from Buddhist, Hindu, and Islamic paths. He had several vivid dreams of Jesus and his interest in the scriptures deepened.

Dave's wife, Gail, first came to the group out of curiosity

when the meetings were held in their home. She initially thought the group was a cult but was drawn in by the members' sharing of their personal difficulties, some of which she could relate to. She began to warm to the group. She liked the idea of not having to agree with subjects that were controversial to her, such as reincarnation. She said that the work she did as part of the group broadened her spiritual outlook, enhanced her dream life, and helped her control her panic attacks.

Bill, another member of the Saratoga group, was volunteering at A.R.E. Camp when he heard a voice tell him, "To be healed, you must heal others." He subsequently studied chiropractic and acupressure, aiding others in need.

Another group member said that her first encounter with the group resulted in "a feeling washing over me that I am home now." She has been grateful for SFG friends with whom she can discuss "the real values in life." She finds a sense of cosmic inner harmony within the group, and, as she looks back, she believes that her response to the Study Group material probably saved her marriage twenty-two years ago.

Ruth, the oldest member at 80, said that belonging to a group gave her a sense of feeling grounded and steadied.

Sandy said that the group helped her change her image of God from a harsh and judgmental creator to a loving and merciful One. But now she isn't uncomfortable with how others perceive God. "God does not require me to understand Him on anyone else's terms, only my own. The study group experience can't be put into words. It must be experienced."

Another member, Linda, said that by hearing how others struggle in trying to follow the ways of Jesus, she sees her own problems in new ways, is able to find the face of God in her friends, and expands her capacity for empathy. She believes that she has become more love-filled and godlike through learning to accept and love others—in the Study Group and beyond it. She thinks the group has an "energy of sharing" and that she has experienced spiritual

highs at some of the group's meditations. "These carry over
into the week and help me be more patient and loving."

Her husband, Mike, who had begun daily prayers for
others through the A.R.E.'s Northeast region Power of
Prayer network, began to realize the healing effect of this
practice on himself. "I am all too familiar with excuses for
not meditating. But now I have a volunteer job where those
on the prayer list depend on me." He found that his meditations were becoming deeper "perhaps because of getting
out of self and attending to the needs of others."

Another member, Judy, summed up the impact that
Study Group has had on her. "Our group task was to bring
God into all our interactions with others. I struggled with
this, but at the next group meeting, I was given a vision that
pictorially showed me the place I was in when God was included in my interactions. It was a place of safety that allowed me to stay open to 'that of God' in folks around me.
Now, when I need it, I can call up that image and instantly
be transported to that sacred place."

Bill sees "enormous potential" in the Search for God
group. He keeps the group's experiments in mind whenever he meets people. "I certainly wasn't always successful.
I would have my victories, then would forget myself when
my mouth would get the better of me. Nevertheless, the
experiments kept a certain spiritual lesson in front of me.
If I am going to search for God, then I will find God in each
person I encounter, each day. Naturally, the one I met most
often was myself."

Sheryl called on her fellow members for special prayers
to be healed of a lifelong phobia of dogs. In addition to support from the group, a dream aided her in overcoming that
fear. "Being a member of this group is like having an inner
well filled with stories of hope, compassion, fun, and wisdom gained from pain," she said.

Graham, the author, said that the Study Group disciplines had enhanced his ability to see God in others. "After
all these years of sharing *A Search for God*, disciplines,
meditation, and refreshments, it is most gratifying to real-

ize that together we have woven a circle of caring. We have become part of each others' journeys. Like facets of a diamond, we each add sparkle to the jewel that is our group. Jesus said, 'I call you not servants . . . but I have called you friends.' We have become friends."

* * *

Carla grew up with an interest in plants. She remembers as a child being introduced to a sensitive plant, a member of the mimosa family. When its leaves are touched, they curl into a tight cylinder. The energy amazed her.

She was also a writer at an early age. In her teens she came across a stack of her mother's *Writer's Digest* magazines, one of the resources for freelance writers, and she began to write. At sixteen she had her first article—about plants—published. At seventeen she was writing a gardening column for a local newspaper.

At that time, Carla's mother was interested in Edgar Cayce and other metaphysical teachings, and soon Carla found herself drawn to similar concepts.

A dream when she was twenty-two brought a major change in her life. In the dream she went to hug a man lying in a hospital bed, and as she did, he pushed her away. She awoke crying, but the image of the man in her dream remained with her.

A short time later, she had a blind date. When her escort for the evening arrived at her front door, she realized that he was the man in her dream. "I knew on that first date that we were going to be married. I felt I had known him forever. We met in August 1983 and after four or five dates, we got married on September 12."

She became the mother to an instant brood of children, her husband's four offspring, ages twelve to eighteen. She learned motherhood quickly, and the family's life was happy and fun.

But when the youngest child finally left home and her husband was spending much time at his work, she began to feel lost. Alone much of the time and not writing much, she began to meditate on her own. It helped and she began to notice positive changes.

Along with the changes came a desire to join the A.R.E., which she did. Then she felt a strong urge to join a Study Group. Unable to locate one in proximity to her home, she started the Somerville, Ohio, Group #1.

There was another change along the way, this one as the result of a youngster's challenge with her first name. Her grandson couldn't pronounce "Carla." The closest he could come was "Carry." She changed one letter—the second *a* to *y*: Carly—and it seemed that things began to fall into place. Her writing, which had been collecting rejection slips, began to be accepted. Her meditations began to help her creatively. "When I was writing, it was almost as if it wasn't my idea. I was guided subconsciously."

Returning to one of her first loves, plants, she authored *Flower Secrets Revealed*, which was published. Another book followed, then a third.

When she looks back at the past fifteen years, she believes that her decision to meditate was the turning point in her life.

"I've come to depend on it. I don't always get to it every day on my own, but the group meditation at our Monday Study Group really helps me focus and see the next step from wherever I am."

* * *

Beth looked squarely into the face of a life crisis.

Asthmatic attacks had forced her into a hospital several times a year for the past seven years. She had just met with her doctor who told her, "There's nothing more I can do for you." She was already on the best medication available, but her condition was worsening. She felt as though the doctor had pronounced a death sentence.

When Beth arrived home and saw her seven-year-old daughter, the tears began to flow. "I wasn't ready to go. My daughter still needed me; and I needed to see her grow up."

As she stood at the kitchen sink after dinner, looking out at her meditation garden, she offered up a healing prayer. When the answer came, she heard the words, "Seek instead a closer walk with God."

First surprised, then excited, she went out the next day and bought a long-playing spiritual recording which included the song, "A Closer Walk With God." As she was listening to the song the next day, the postman delivered a membership book from the A.R.E. It was *A Search for God, Book I.*

The following morning, Beth's sister called. She had been communicating with A.R.E. about Study Groups in the area, had received back the addresses of two groups, and wanted to know if Beth would join a group with her. Beth agreed.

Once in the group, Beth began working on dreams for guidance. Soon thereafter her husband joined. They began to build a library of Cayce and A.R.E. books, and she and her husband started meditating as a family and exploring the benefits of holistic health, using a variety of remedies and preventives.

Beth began to work with her attitudes and emotions. As she learned to meditate better, she began to learn more patience, and inspirational messages began to come to her through meditation and dreams.

Without noticing it at first, her health began to improve. Soon she stopped taking medication for her high blood pressure. Next the Valium was set aside as she began to achieve restful sleep on her own.

The asthma attacks stopped, and Beth became a stranger to the hospital. "I have been too busy learning to be a channel of blessings to others and trying to see good in everyone and every situation I meet."

The relationship between Beth and her husband also improved as they turned inward to solve their differences and found better and more lasting solutions than they could have imagined.

They became members of two Study Groups, following one of the members of the original group when she started a new group in a downtown area. They went with her to help her start the group process, but enjoyed it so much that they stayed.

"We see so much good happening to people who apply spiritual laws to their lives."

*   *   *

The phone call was the beginning of a remarkable experience.

Jackie's friend from a Search for God Study Group had urgency in her voice when she spoke. "My grandmother is terminally ill in the hospital with pneumonia. I would like her name put on the prayer list, but I don't think it should be for healing. She's ninety-seven years old, and I think she needs help to make the transition."

Jackie agreed, and the grandmother's name was put on both women's Study Groups' prayer lists and the region's Glad Helpers network.

Mary's grandmother had been in declining health for a number of years; a number of small strokes had resulted in partial paralysis and impaired comprehension and concentration. After church on Thanksgiving morning, Jackie agreed to help Mary make the seven-hour drive to her grandmother.

Despite warnings of snow and freezing rain, the two had a pleasant drive and reached Mary's grandmother in late afternoon. The elderly woman had suffered another stroke, was unable to speak, and conveyed an indifferent attitude when they tried to make her more comfortable.

At dinner the two women discussed what could be done to ease the transition. Mary thought of her son Ted, who had died in an automobile accident six years earlier. He was the only one who had been on good terms with her grandmother. The elderly woman had dominated the family and given them little reason to want to assist her. Jackie wondered whether her own daughter, who had passed over nine years earlier, might help. A psychic reading for Jackie some weeks earlier had said that the daughter was working with small children since she crossed over. At that point Jackie just turned the need over to God.

The next morning the two Study Group members shared their guidances from the previous night. Jackie's daughter had come to her and said she wanted very much to help the grandmother and that it would give her great joy. She confirmed to Jackie that she had helped mostly accident victims to cross over and most of them thought of her as an angel. She said it would be fine if the grandmother wanted to think of her as an angel, too.

Mary said that her son had come to her to express his willingness to help his great-grandmother make the transition. The son had come in the form of a knowing and a presence following her prayer.

The grandmother was alert when the two arrived. The two women told the older one that Jesus loved her and that the Creator made and loved her and that she deserved such love, that it was all right to let go of her body and cross over whenever she was ready. They told her that the two children were on the other side ready to help lead her to the light.

The two returned after lunch to find that the doctor had adjusted downward the intravenous flow. They again talked with the grandmother about her being loved and everyone wanting only to help her.

But the woman lying in the bed was looking beyond them. It was then that Jackie sensed a movement. She sensed the presence of the two children. "That's your great-grandson, and my daughter is behind him. They're waiting to help you whenever you are ready. You only have to reach out, and they will help you to cross over and lead you to the light."

The elderly woman turned and looked in wonder.

The two women drove back home. When Jackie awoke the following morning, she sensed her daughter's presence and kept a prayerful attitude for several hours. Her daughter's presence faded around 10 a.m. About noon, Jackie's friend called and said, "Grandma passed on at 9:30 this morning."

Later Mary said that she had felt the strong presence of her son and Jackie's daughter and of both her deceased parents. She said she believed that Jackie and her daughter would work together in the future to help those who needed assistance in transition.

Jackie was reminded of a series of dreams she had years earlier, after her daughter's death. The dreams told her that her mission in the decade of the nineties was to help those who were not prepared to pass over.

*   *   *

Tom's Study Group was discussing one of the principles of dealing with an unpleasant problem: the only way to get rid of it is to face it, study it, solve it, and overcome it.

As the discussion went on, Tom's thoughts returned to his work as a twenty-five-year-old engineer who was very unhappy in his work. The more unhappy he became, the more he avoided his responsibility by taking walks around the plant, talking about his work instead of doing it, and stretching out the assignments.

It was about this time that his boss, an acknowledged atheist, pointed out that if Tom were really a Christian, he would fulfill his duty to work diligently in order to give his employer his money's worth. Tom knew he was right.

For the next three months, Tom worked on adopting an attitude that his job, although he still disliked it, was the best job in the world, that it wasn't a job at all, but instead was really play. It wasn't easy for him; he had a lot of talks with himself, but the harder he tried, the easier it became.

Once he was able to solve the work-attitude problem, he was offered a much better job with a different company. "I have been convinced, since the Search for God realization, that if I had not tackled my attitudinal problem, that call would never have reached me."

In his new job, Tom saw older men racing to leave work each day, a clear indication that they were as unhappy as he had been. He began thinking about those men and others in similar situations.

Years after his self-discovery was reinforced in his Search for God Study Group, he shared some of his hard-earned wisdom:

"Perhaps a good way to start making change is to adopt the style some call *intentional living*. Intentional living is a mental approach that says, 'I will make a positive decision about the things I do or do not do. I will stop reacting with guilt feelings about things I am not doing because I know that what I am doing is more important to me right now.'

"We have been talking about freedom—freedom to do, freedom from reaction. In searching for the seemingly unconscious mental chains that bind us and attacking them one at a time until they are broken, we make life more and more fun—much like a treasure hunt. But instead of finding physical treasures that add to our load, we find mental treasures that lighten it. As we discard them, one at a time, our available energy grows along with our sense of an expanding life—and we can thank our Creator for helping us in our quest."

*   *   *

Like so many others, Dick can look back at past years and see how far he has come in his transformation. It has been a gradual process that has changed his life and there have been many catalysts, including his work with a Study Group.

Dick's background was in traditional religion. His father was a minister and Dick's early years were rooted in the Methodist Church. In his late thirties he began to develop a strong interest in the unexplainable: ghosts, psychic ability, UFOs. In spite of a scientific background—degrees in mathematics and physics—he began to read about "these strange things that might be true."

His church attendance and his prayer life had lapsed, but he felt a need to redefine his view of God.

Along the way Dick came to accept that "the psychic is basically of a spiritual nature and to be used in a spiritual way," he said. "I became convinced of a relationship between the psychic and a thing we honor as God." He also came to feel that the church's usual approach to Christ is earthbound. "I like to think that Christ and God are universal, or cosmic, forces."

In the late sixties, he came across *The Sleeping Prophet*, and when he had finished the book, he knew he had to become involved in the Cayce work. Once involved, he began to ponder the concept of reincarnation, and, as a result, a friend suggested he might be comfortable within the family of the Unity Church. When he moved to Dallas in the mid-seventies, Dick relinquished his membership in the Methodist Church and began his affiliation with Unity.

As he continued to look for answers to his life, he found them in a Study Group with Elsie Sechrist, whose reputation as a dream interpreter was well known throughout the nation as a result of her book *Dreams: Your Magic Mirror*. Dick began to receive guidance through dreams and his meditations.

In one dream, he saw himself putting on his father's blue suit, the one his Dad wore for his Sunday services. The coat was too big. He asked himself, "Dick, are you really spiritually mature enough to take on more spiritual responsibility?" To answer that question, he followed a lingering idea he had held and enrolled in Atlantic University, polishing his own spiritual growth and becoming the first person to complete the university's home-study master's degree program.

Dick has continued to follow the guidance he receives. "I just plan to make myself available and see what unfolds." Now a certified Unity teacher, he also authored an important book for A.R.E., *The Edgar Cayce Bible Companion*.

Some of the guidance that mapped out Dick's course and perhaps his continuing life purpose had its origin in a Texas

Study Group, where he began to understand the power of dreams.

* * *

Tina, stationed in Virginia Beach for a decade as a librarian in the Navy, spent a lot of time in the A.R.E. library. What she learned there would become her foundation when she moved to Jersey City to begin a job as a social worker helping families of alcoholics.

Eventually, the pressures of raising three children ended the job, and she turned her concentration toward her family and herself. For years, Tina had been aware that her hands often became hot, and her heritage, passed down in stories from her elders, made her think that heat might be evil.

As a result, she enrolled in a workshop, "Empowering Yourself to Heal," and soon Tina's life began to change. When the workshop leader placed her hands on Tina's shoulders, Tina felt an enormous power "like God's power," she recalled. "At that moment I was at complete peace. When I left the seminar that day, I knew I had to do something."

She opened her home to her neighbors, inviting them to bring their children over on occasion for "A Healing Place." "There's great despair where I live," she said. "So many parents are single and don't have enough time or money to care for their children the way they'd like to. Some need help with relationships."

Tina and her neighbors began to come together through fellowship, prayer, discussions of metaphysics, and working with children. Tina herself was able to help a small boy begin to overcome his speech difficulty and was instrumental in helping a little girl avoid an operation to correct a hearing impediment.

"The Healing Place" took hold, and soon twenty-five people were meeting every Wednesday and Thursday evening.

In December of that year, Tina and her visitors formed into a regular A.R.E. Study Group that met weekly. Out of those meetings has come a new direction for the former Navy librarian. "Whenever I pray and meditate, I ask God to lead me to use the opportunities and abilities He gives me. Now I feel so blessed because I have a chance to serve. I can help people learn more about God so their lives can be better."

* * *

Martha, a charter member of a Study Group that was founded in 1962, perhaps best sums up the essence of Study Group work that has been vital to her transformation.

"The most important thing that brings transformation is fellowship. We're all lonesome when we haven't found our place yet. We need someone to talk to about these things. It's not just the information that is important. I've gone over it so many times. I'm going to Study Group to be with people. With every group, you're going to meet yourself in some new way. The important thing is being with people who are working at being transformed," she said.

The changes in her life have been gradual but easily measurable. She was a quiet, private child, very uncomfortable with strangers. She worked through her teen years in an effort to become more outgoing and more popular. As a result, she became unsure of what her belief system really was. College psychology courses further confounded her. "There was no room for the mystic," a feeling that was part of her Scottish heritage. Challenged and unhappy, she asked God for evidence of His presence.

Shortly thereafter, she read about *There Is A River* in the *Saturday Review* and began reading and studying the Cayce material on her own, before there were Study Groups in her area.

Her marriage to a fellow student and the arrival of four daughters brought much of the Cayce material into active practice in her life. "The A.R.E. has been very instrumental in my life. I don't know how I would have coped with marriage and children without it. In a family, you confront yourself in so many ways. I can look back now and see the difference in myself. Even being married to someone who seemed to have a similar background, I would sometimes find a person coming from a totally different spot than I ever imagined. That's when the readings on knowing yourself and cooperating became so important. When my husband died after twenty years of marriage, I realized that it was working, beginning to be a success."

Whenever her Study Group is working on the "Ideals" chapter in *A Search for God*, she spends time and thought in reviewing her own ideals, and now, for the woman who was a private child, those ideals include others:

"Gradually, over the years, especially by working with the Cayce information, my sense of separateness eroded, and I learned the importance of being helpful and productive in other people's lives, not just my own. Now I feel that we are like the tips of the fingers on the right and left hands. We might think we are separate, but we are all one being."

Chapter 7

FROM THE FILES: STUDY GROUPS

*I joined A.R.E. Many books and tapes later I helped orga-
nize a Search for God Study Group called "Salmon #1."
Though small in numbers, we are reaping great things. The
greatest for me was to find God walking by my side, a friend,
not a vindictive judge, and that discovery changed my entire approach to life, including the way I talk to Him.*

*   *   *

*Twenty-one years ago, I stopped at a small cafe in Custer,
Wyoming, spotted a book in the rack, and read it all the way
home. The book:* The Miracle Man of Virginia Beach. *It
changed my life.*

*For me, A.R.E. clarifies the reality of things. Our purposes
in the earth and our opportunities together all come alive
as I read the Cayce material.*

*The most enriching times are with my Study Group . . . I've
seen miracles happen over the years.*

*   *   *

*I was working as an office temp, reading a book on mysti-
cism during lunch breaks. A co-worker asked if I'd like to
visit a meeting about some Edgar Cayce Study Groups here*

in town. The group we visited, Eastlake #1, became my second home for three years. I met Brent during a group meeting, and we married with our group in attendance. I think we most respond to the integrity we find in the Cayce readings. I can't imagine my life without the A.R.E. friends we know and the knowledge and experience we have gained from the Cayce readings.

* * *

Words cannot convey my profound gratitude to God for Edgar Cayce's life and work and for all those who seek to make it live in their own lives.

My entire life has been transformed as a result of eighteen years in Study Group, and I look forward to the profound transformations still to come. This work truly has life only when it is lived.

Chapter 8

WHERE PRAYERS ARE ANSWERED

It's a small office, kept neat despite constant activity, on the second floor of the Cayce Hospital building. From this cubicle each month nearly 4,000 people throughout the world are connected in healing prayer for hundreds who have requested help. Meredith Puryear, who occupies the space as A.R.E.'s prayer coordinator, has been working with the Glad Helpers, as the healing prayer group is most often known, since 1969.

She is guardian of a legacy that began in September 1931, when Edgar Cayce had a dream. Cayce gave this account of the dream in a reading (294-127) for himself on September 15, 1931:

The Norfolk Group were gathered for the reading on their first lesson. (295) sat down by my side, laid her hand on mine and spoke to the group—saying that, with their permission and mine, she would tell them what the reading was going to tell each of them to do. (560) said, "Well, (295), I've been expecting that all the time. (295) said, "Have you?" She answered, "I certainly have." Then all the group laughed. (295) seemed set back, not knowing whether to go on or not. She asked me if she should go on and I said, "Certainly, if you have anything to tell them, go ahead." Then she began to tell them.

I don't remember what she told each to do, except that she said, "We will have a healing circle. (993) will be the leader, (560) will be the interpreter of what each want and how the circle is to pray for the individual, and we will have spiritual healing." She chose (993), Mrs. (69), Mrs. (2112), Mr. (2124), (341), and (560). (993) insisted that (295) should be the leader, but (295) said that (993) should be the leader.

Then I saw a place I had never seen before. (295) was doing the talking, and they were trying to decide as to which hour was the hour for prayer. (295) said, "We will have prayer twice each day, at seven o'clock in the morning and at six o'clock in the evening." They all said they couldn't be there twice a day all the time, and (295) said, "If we are in earnest, we will be here— and that's the correct time. Some said, "Well, that's the Mohammedan hour of prayer." (295) said, "I know it, but that's the right time."

Then I saw them preparing the breathing exercises and the manner in which they were to act for that particular thing that (560) pointed out which they were to do, and (295) was leading them.

His reading continued:

This, as has been seen, is as the promise that was given that each in his or her individual way and manner would be *given* a vision, a message, as to his or her part or portion in the undertaking to which the group—*as* a group; individuals, *as* individuals—had pledged themselves.

As indicated, there had been left a most important part of a program that should be *begun* with the studies undertaken from time to time. In not seeing what each was to give to the particular *lesson,* they *were* each to determine and ask in their own way, for their *own* enlightenment.

As seen, the body could lead in that portion or part

of the work, aided and abetted by those who were seen in the vision as it happened.

Well, then, that this group—when others have given, or sought to know their part—that this group as seen, the seven, be given that as an *additional* portion of their part in the work.

To be sure this will be altered as to meeting, as to times, yet eventually this group may hold—with even *thousands* of others—such a prayer for those who are sick or afflicted in any manner, and they to whom the will is given will receive that they seek through the efforts of these who were with Him.

The reading ended with Cayce's familiar closing words, "We are through," and the healing prayer group, conceived out of the original Search for God Study Group, was born.

Less than a month after the members of the first Study Group had received their initial reading from Edgar Cayce in which they sought guidance in their undertaking, the members of the healing group gathered in the office of the seer to ask the questions of "why" and "how" for their endeavor:

GC: We, the group designated as the healing group have gathered here to seek through these channels to know why and how we are fitted to carry on this special part of the work. Please guide us into the right path, that we may know Thy Will and be used to do Thy Work.

EC: Yes, we have the group as gathered here, as designated as a group to carry on that portion in this material world. Each as are gathered here are fitted in their own particular way for a portion of that work designated by the group as the healing group. Hence, when once chosen, and the face set in that direction, that as the warning, as the threat.

In each experience of the individuals gathered here, they—the individuals—have contacted various other individuals in experiences in life, some for weal, some for woe, as has been designated to each in those experiences where either development or retardment has been the portion of that individual experience. As these individuals, then, have contacted others, these have that karma, that experience to be worked out together for some definite purpose other than that of self-indulgence, self-gratification, or self-exaltation. In some this has been the last experience. Hence there is seen that there will be those characterizations in the associations when turned to earthly conditions. Then there are those experiences with the group as a whole where the greater portion have worked together for the common good of all. Then are those contacts where there was healing brought in their individual experience with the divine forces manifested in a material world. Then again the group as a whole in the dispensing of an ideal as was designated in a material plane through that leading of one through whom sources of information may be given to each, that will assist and aid in all phases of their experience in the present. Then, as may be seen, *these* are the ways, the *manners*, in which each are fitted—and fitting themselves, by the one common purpose—to be a manifestation of His love in this particular experience. As they fit themselves in their respective niches in this ideal, this purpose, this aim, are *these—as* a group—*designated* as those who, with an individual, may lose self in love and service to others. 281-1

In the formative years, nearly everyone in the entire group obtaining the Study Group readings had elected to become part of and work with the prayer healing group. But there were growing pains as the members wrestled with dual commitments. Within the first year, the healing group, now known as the Glad Helpers, sought a reading on September 7, 1932, to understand the difficulties:

(Q) Please explain why the healing group (281) has

been unable to make its work clear to the study group (262)?

(A) Differences of opinions in the activities of individuals, or personality and individuality clashing over material points when the spiritual and mental should be the basis for all considerations.

In these variations, well that all should consider that attempting to be accomplished, rather than by whom or what is being used for the accomplishing of that ideal; letting *Him* be the guide, forgetting self or self's feelings, or self's interests in any manner; for, as He gave, "I do nothing of myself."

(Q) How may this be done?

(A) Just as given, "I do nothing of myself." Let others do as they will or may, but for myself I will be led as *He* directs.

(Q) Is it best that the healing group give up their readings that there may be more harmony in the study group?

(A) This depends upon the purpose of the healing group. Are they to be ruled or governed by individuals' ideas, or they to be used in His service as *He* would direct? 281-11

It was this last answer in the reading that has endured as the unshakable foundation for the Glad Helpers, as well as for all other endeavors associated with The Work: to be used in His service as He would direct.

The work of the healing prayer group, which continued to seek advice through the readings, began to receive reports that their efforts were aiding and transforming lives. In the February 1933 *A.R.E. Bulletin*, Hugh Lynn Cayce reported to the membership, "Many encouraging reports and letters have been received, and each (member) feel their efforts have been far-reaching in effect.

"Three periods of meditation are kept daily by the Glad Helpers, and those seeking aid are asked to hold at least one of these periods. All affirmations used by the group are obtained through the readings, and the group's work is at all times guided by counsel from these sources. Anyone having faith in the Divine Force within and without who feels the need of such service as this group may render is invited to communicate . . . "

Gladys Davis, Cayce's young stenographer who had quickly grasped the importance of The Work and who was a member of the healing group, explained to the Second A.R.E. Congress on June 18, 1933, the purpose and the work of the Glad Helpers. She demonstrated rare insight into the efforts of the then-small group as they worked to change others' lives for the better:

> The Glad Helpers is a prayer group within the Norfolk Study Group No. 1, which is open to those who seek through it. I think the purpose is very well signified by the name—Glad Helpers. We *are* glad helpers. It is our purpose to help individuals, physically and mentally, by attempting through meditation to awaken the divine within each. We have been told through a reading by Mr. Cayce that the spiritual is the life, the mental is the builder, and the physical is the result. Therefore, no healing of any nature, mental or physical, can take place without an awakening of the inner or spiritual self.
>
> We have three periods of meditation each day, and we ask all to join us who have the desire to aid in bringing peace, harmony, light and immortality to others, through the raising of the Christ Consciousness within and projecting it to others. We believe that Jesus, the Christ, has shown the perfect Way, He has laid the foundation, He has reached perfection; but we must raise ourselves and overcome the carnal forces even as He, in order to reach the perfection towards which we should all be striving. We believe He taught that every inharmony, every suffering, is a result of disobedience to divine laws: not a punishment direct from God, but a natural result of our own acts. Earthly

parents might try very hard to impress upon their child that it must not do a certain thing or it will suffer thereby. But if the child goes ahead anyway, then it must suffer the consequences. The parents can help, but the child must learn the lesson. Jesus, the Christ, through having overcome, has made the way easy. He has blazed the trail. We only have to tune in to His Consciousness to be free from all earthly woes. No matter how straight and narrow the path, we can hew to it with His help.

So, it is our purpose to try, through meditation—and also through our thoughts, words and acts day by day—to break down those barriers which have been builded between the material and spiritual, and project into those vacant places the love, peace and understanding that may cause perfect harmony.

The higher we are able to raise the Christ Consciousness within us, the more we are able to project it outward and direct it to certain individuals who are seeking. If those individuals are in attune at the time, they catch it immediately. If not, there may be a delay in their receiving it, but the good is not lost. It goes out into the ether, and adds to the constructive influences that are building towards perfect harmony and peace.

For the next eleven years, the Glad Helpers sought periodic guidance and new affirmations from The Work as they met, prayed, and healed. By 1974, the sixty-five readings given for the group had been assembled into a single volume, *Meditation, Part I*, of the *Edgar Cayce Library Series*. By that year, thousands of people across the world were keeping the prayer time, and testimonials to the effectiveness of prayer and the transformation of countless lives had been received by A.R.E.

Meredith Ann Puryear, A.R.E.'s present prayer group coordinator, joined the healing prayer group in 1969. She had been especially focused on the Cayce readings about prayer, meditation, and healing, as well as the Palestine period and Bible history.

Her devotion to healing prayer and her constant study of The Work resulted in the publication in 1978 of her book, *Healing Through Prayer and Meditation,* which has been instrumental to individuals in helping to transform their fellow beings.

Her commitment to healing others prompted her to share her knowledge and her experiences. In 1980, she authored a two-part series on spiritual healing for the *A.R.E. Journal.* The series was a benefit to those who had an interest in a more enlightened way to heal themselves and a troubled world. In part, she wrote:

"Edgar Cayce did not give just a purely physical reading or a life reading without referring to principles that would encompass the total being (entity) of a person; for the entity to be really healthy, the physical, mental, and spiritual dimensions always needed to be brought into balance.

"Therefore, a definition of health, and the healing needed to bring it about, might be this: Health is the attunement of the physical, mental, and spiritual to the Divine, producing within the entity health and manifesting outwardly as lover in relationship to others."

The readings state it this way:

> You see, it is not that there are just so many treatments to be given and they can all be gotten through with and that's all there is to it! *No* application of *any* medicinal property or any mechanical adjustment, or any other influence, is healing of itself! These applications merely help to attune, adjust, correlate the activities of the bodily functions to nature and natural sources!
>
> All healing, then, is from life! Life is God! 2153-6

Chapter 9

FROM THE FILES: GLAD HELPERS

I am writing to thank all of you for your prayers in my behalf. I know they have helped. God has blessed me with much less physical pain and an understanding of my emotional pain. I believe both are finally healing.

Since the Glad Helpers have started including my name on their prayer list, I have found a doctor that has helped me with my physical pain. There is no cure yet, but maybe in the next few years there will be.

My emotional scar started healing with the miracle of finding my daughter after thirty years. I don't think I will ever get over this miracle. Each time I think of it I can't help but know it was with the help of your prayers and God's knowing what it was that I really needed in my life. I was asking for a physical healing. God went one better. He healed my mind and heart and, in a way, my soul. I can't tell you how profoundly grateful I am, and I feel blessed.

Please do continue your good work there at A.R.E. The Glad Helpers are a tremendous help.

* * *

Since you put me on the prayer list and did a laying on of hands there for me, I have begun my recovery.

On January 1, I took my first steps in over two weeks, and

I walk slowly now—even outside for short distances.

As painful and relentless as this illness has been, the trea-sures, from dreams, visions, and new understanding, more than compensate.

I see the world through new eyes, and somehow—all my perceptions about life, what I believed about what is good and who God is, were wiped away, leaving me empty in the best sense. I am open to the mystery and inner revelation which was promised and which is our heritage as His chil-dren. Until this illness cleared me out, I did not know how blocked I was by my beliefs gathered over a lifetime.

Thank you and your circle of healers who do so much good for so many in need.

*   *   *

I just wanted to write and thank you for your support and tell you that I believe that your prayers helped tremendously during the death of my son three days before Christmas and also for me personally when I appeared in person before you and asked for prayers to heal my psoriasis when I was there in early November for the psoriasis conference. My psoriasis has cleared up since I was there for the conference and so far has not broken out again. Thank God. I personally believe that a permanent healing may have been accomplished, in part thanks to all your prayers. During the shock of my son's death, I could feel the support and help being given from above again, thanks to your prayers.

When I am next at the Beach, I will try and stop to thank you personally, but I wanted to write and say how very much your prayers helped. May God bless each one of you.

*   *   *

Thank you—thank the Glad Helpers for sending the prayer list each month. Not only do I appreciate the oppor-tunity and the privilege of praying for those who seek prayer, but your letter, your comments, your tried and trusted sug-

gestions have been, and still are, of such great help to me personally.

Our Study Group continues to wonder at the way we are given new insights all the time. Our understanding of the material in the readings is forever growing and expanding— an ongoing learning experience and there seems to be no end to it. I don't think I expected this to be the case with prayer— but it is!

*　　*　　*

I just wanted to let you all know that my friend and partner has remarkably and quite miraculously improved. I know it is due to your prayers along with ours. He had been in the hospital for almost six months, near death for a while, when the prayers were started. He had a severe case of pneumonia, a secondary infection in lungs and urinary tract, aspiration problems, prostate infection (on which they were going to operate), anemia, a stomach condition, an irregular heart beat, and a loss of thirty-five pounds. We thought we would lose him.

A few weeks into the prayers, he began to improve. He is now eating well, walking without a cane, showing no sign of infection, requiring no operation, driving, and has gained back twenty-five pounds. One more month of prayer, whenever you can put him on the list, will be appreciated.

What a miracle! Thanks to you, all of you.

*　　*　　*

Dad passed his last swallow test on December 2 and subsequently was discharged from the home care agency, so there are no more visiting nurses or aides. He has been on a soft diet ever since and is doing wonderfully with it—no aspiration. By decreasing his formula slightly each week, we were able to wean him off the feeding pump and ship the contraption back to the medical supply company.

Dad is also walking without the walker now and is walk-

ing steadier and straighter, though he still needs assistance because of his cataracts.

We both know it's the prayers that have made all the difference and ask that you please keep our names on the Prayer List, that He will continue His healing work in us both.

*   *   *

I just wish to thank you for doing what you do. I put my son on the emergency list a couple of weeks ago. I felt like he really needed the extra energy of prayer from people like yourselves.

I am also remembering the people on the prayer list every day.

As soon as the prayers began, things got better. He is getting back to living and not being depressed. It was a situation he had never been faced with and didn't know how to handle—and was letting his life fall apart. Again, thank you so much. It is wonderful to know there is a place to turn and where I felt the difference immediately. Bless you.

Chapter 10

BEYOND THE BEACH

The gatherings were modest at first.

Shortly after the Cayce Hospital opened at Virginia Beach in February 1929, Edgar Cayce and Morton Blumenthal, the major benefactor of the hospital, began offering Sunday evening lectures on aspects of The Work. Members of the National Association of Investigators and local residents would attend to hear Cayce explain the information that came through the readings.

The Sunday lecture series was a modest foreshadowing of the association's modern-day conferences that reach out to individuals across the nation and across the world and that have been the first step toward transformation for thousands of individuals.

Although the hospital closed in 1931, the lectures continued and the National Association of Investigators became the Association for Research and Enlightenment in the same year. Cayce gave readings for the organization at its annual Congress—the yearly gathering of the membership—and lectured on The Work, its application to individuals, and how it could benefit others. Hugh Lynn Cayce, who accepted the challenge of leadership after his father's death, took the lectures about The Work to the people. Often alone or sometimes with a person who had come to benefit from The Work, he traveled back and forth across the country, building a solid foundation for the educational outreach of the A.R.E.

The small lecture hall in the Wynne Building in Virginia Beach gave way to the Library/Conference Center in 1975, and the A.R.E. staff members were joined by nationally known and respected speakers in presenting weeklong conferences that examined The Work and how it might be applied in people's lives.

For nearly seventy years, in small halls and modern conference facilities around the world, individuals have come to learn, and many have left to walk a different, more meaningful path.

*　*　*

John was at a crossroads that many young people face.

A college degree and an interest in international business had led only to a job as a waiter. Seeking out a different direction, he talked with a relative who had introduced his parents to the Cayce material. Although he was thinking of a possible move to California because of its varied spiritual offerings, the relative encouraged him to look more closely at the Cayce material.

An earlier experience in India, when he was traveling alone, had fortified John's growing desire to live a more spiritually centered life.

On a quest to see the Dalai Lama, he was felled by dysentery in the foothills of the Himalayas.

After two months of walking alone through India, he found himself exhausted, with no place for the night and with no help at hand.

He let go of all of his human control and turned his dire situation over to God. When he opened his eyes, he saw a young Indian boy walk by. The youngster came over to him and asked, "Place to sleep?"

Following the boy over steep and rough terrain, John finally collapsed. The boy picked up his backpack and urged John on to the boy's modest home. For three days, the family helped John recover and he became part of a celebration of his rescuer's sixteenth birthday, highlighted by a village ceremony.

When he left India, John felt that he had truly been connected to the Source, the Christ Spirit in India.

It was with this feeling that he turned to the A.R.E., at his relative's suggestion.

His call to the A.R.E. led him to a "Finding Your Mission in Life" conference. As a result of the course, he learned that his mission was "to be a peacemaker in the world through deepening spiritual values in [himself] and others."

Jayne, an A.R.E. member from Pittsburgh, also attended the conference. She had seen John in a dream before the conference and knew that he would serve as an excellent role model for young people.

She asked if he'd be interested in working with a teen rite-of-passage program called "The Journey," which she believed could be blended with material in the readings and experiences at the A.R.E. Camp.

Her question led John to a new direction in his life. "When Jayne told me about 'The Journey,' I recalled feeling a quick surge of energy pass through me, a feeling that in India I had learned to understand as a message from Spirit."

He left his job as a waiter and moved to Virginia Beach, where he joined the A.R.E. staff. Initially, he worked with the prison program, Study Groups, and education. He assisted with camp programs and became a "Journey" facilitator, developing a creative approach to the "necessary crises of adolescence."

Today, he is an integral part of the A.R.E. Conferences staff. He helps plan, facilitate, and make available to others the kinds of educational insights about The Work that helped him find his path as a peacemaker.

*   *   *

Patty, Gordon, and their respective spouses had become friends after an unplanned meeting. Gordon was a retired Army colonel and city building official. Patty's husband was in construction. Their jobs brought the two men together, and the four evolved into close friends.

Sadness, however, visited both families. Gordon lost his wife of forty-three years to cancer, and Patty, who had been a student of various spiritual teachings, found her marriage failing and became a divorcee.

The two began to go on dates, including a visit to Unity, at Patty's suggestion. It was at a Unity group that Gordon was able to revisit an unhappy childhood with an abusive and alcoholic father. He began to understand the origin of his hard-nosed approach to many situations.

With encouragement from Patty, Gordon began to change his attitude, and they married. Both became leaders in Unity and other spirit-based groups. For the first time, Patty had a mate who was interested in metaphysical studies and spiritual growth.

In 1992, the two attended an A.R.E. conference, "Discovering Your Soul's Purpose," in Kansas City, Missouri. It was Gordon's first A.R.E. seminar, and the two of them came away with a renewed sense of purpose.

"We became more focused on having a purpose in life after that seminar," Patty said. "I discovered that my purpose is 'to be the unconditional love and joy that I am.' Now that the fast-track 'doing' part of our life is past, we are in the 'being' part. We can be our mission in so many small ways every day, like paying compliments to people and helping them feel good."

The result of the seminar for Gordon was a focus on harmony. "Just tuning in to Patty helped me be more harmonious with people."

The two have discovered numerous ways to fulfill their purposes: "Not correcting or finding fault, but trying to bring out the best in the other, as Cayce recommended. Focusing on the positives, like love, kindness, and joy. Being a complement to each other," Patty said.

"Gordon was still a colonel when we first married, but I don't salute colonels. When you're not tender and kind, that can just break my heart."

* * *

Coni was looking for something more. For fourteen years she had been a counselor-healer working with Ernest Holmes's Science of Mind. She returned to the Cayce material and in 1993 became a student in an A.R.E. psychic training workshop. "It was absolutely transforming," she said. "I finally understood, saw, and felt everything that was theory before. I moved away from seeing myself in particular to understanding what I have to do in the larger picture—what my soul's path is, not just what I'm doing as a person."

At that first conference, Coni's ride home had to leave early, but Coni didn't worry as she would have in earlier times. She broadcast that she needed a ride and met a fellow conferee who took her as far as the New Jersey train station. When she went into the station to check on the schedule, she learned that a train to New York, her destination, was due to leave in five minutes. Lessons from the conference were being confirmed.

Later, instead of riding the subway to work as she usually did, she decided to ride the bus. When she arrived at the office, a co-worker asked, "How did you get to work? Your subway line is out."

Coni returned to Virginia Beach for additional psychic training sessions, giving her a view of the connections in life and a new understanding. "I don't rely on my five senses to make decisions anymore."

The changes that came about as a result of her attendance at the conferences are reflected in her professional life: training welfare mothers as a staff member of the New York Board of Education and also teaching English as a second language. She holds a bachelor's and a master's, is certified in administration, and was working on her doctorate.

But now she approaches learning and teaching in a different way since her A.R.E. experiences. "In spite of all the credentials, I have to go back to the place where I started— going with my feelings. I think the future of teaching will be completely different. Working with expanded perception, people will learn more quickly and at a deeper level."

Coni says, "Now I have a lot more certainty about things that, logically, I really don't have any way of knowing."

*   *   *

Shelley was introduced to The Work by one of her mentors. She had already been reaching out to help others, prompted by a tragedy that still gripped her. She had come home one evening to discover that her father had taken his life. There was no note and no understandable explanation for why a man with a loving wife, three children, and a good business would end his life.

Shelley began searching for answers. While a graduate student, she trained as a counselor for the campus Women's Center, believing that her father would have lived had he been able to reach out for help. She wanted to provide that help for others who might need to reach out.

Shelley was asked to cofacilitate a workshop on suicide prevention and, in the process, fell in love and married her co-presenter. He encouraged her to pursue her spiritual search for understanding. It was at this time that she was introduced to the Cayce material. After reading books and participating in a number of home research projects, Shelley enrolled in an A.R.E. workshop on connecting with one's higher self.

A guided meditation during that workshop opened the way for healing.

Asked to imagine meeting her spiritual benefactor, Shelley saw hers as a man dressed in a gray cloak, much like a monk. She was told to ask questions and wait for answers. She inquired about the house that she and her husband were about to purchase. As she asked the question, she realized that the two of them were standing on the porch of the new house, a feeling that gave her a sense that she would receive guidance there.

Next Shelley was instructed in the workshop to receive a gift from her envisioned spiritual mentor. When she opened the box that he presented, she saw an iris inside. When she asked what the flower meant, he responded that it was a reminder to always be true to herself. Shelley thought that this was interesting, but not particularly meaningful.

That night, however, when she was at dinner, she noticed a blue iris painted on the dinner plate. The pattern that she and her husband had selected years earlier was called "Wild Iris." Preparing for bed that night, she noticed a plaque on the wall with the saying, "May I always seek new ways to express what I think, what I feel, who I am." The background was covered with irises.

After moving into their new home, she was surprised one day to see groups of wild irises growing in the backyard, apparently planted there by the former owner. She slowly began to understand the significance of the flowers that she had subconsciously been drawn to for years. They seemed to be telling her, "Be who you are—shine like a star! And don't be afraid to share yourself with the world."

A year or so after the workshop, Shelley felt the need for further exploration. Working with Tarot cards, she realized that she frequently drew the hermit card. She realized that he was the monk from her meditation at the A.R.E. workshop. But she still did not know who he was; she'd never seen his face.

Sometime later, she decided to begin counseling with a body harmony and rebirthing practitioner. On her way to the first appointment, she dashed into a market and stopped suddenly in the floral department where a bunch of irises was in plain view. She took them to her session.

As she began talking with the counselor about her father, she continued to gaze at the flowers. When the counselor asked her if she had ever felt her father's presence, it suddenly came to her that he was the monk who had been guiding her since the workshop. He was, she knew, encouraging her to let go of the past and the anger and guilt and become the person God intended for her to be. She realized that her father had never abandoned her and that he had, instead, guided her to her husband, to their home, and to her life's work as a body harmony practitioner, as well as to her true self.

As she looked back on her experiences, she said, "The A.R.E. workshop gave us the opportunity to reconnect and begin the journey home together."

*   *   *

It was the seemingly simple decision of returning a shell to the sand that marked a great change in Eileen's attitude toward all things.

She was approaching her fiftieth birthday and had decided to give herself a two-month period to reflect on her life and her years ahead. Included in the two months was attendance at her first A.R.E. conference, to be followed by time spent on a lovely East Coast beach in a neighboring state.

The conference exceeded her expectations, and she departed feeling blessed by her time with spirit-filled people.

After the conference, Eileen quickly adopted a daily pattern for her days at the beach retreat. She would read from *A Search for God*, work at mastering meditation, write in her dream journal, and then take a long, easy walk along the beach.

Always intrigued by seashells and their colors and designs, she found that her beach offered great possibilities for collecting shells. Her walks were frequently slowed as she leaned down to pick up and sift the sand for shells.

One morning, however, Eileen became frustrated at finding only fragments of beautiful shells. Nonetheless, she decided to collect some of the fragments as a reminder of the fragments of her own self and as an encouragement to treasure the parts even as she worked toward wholeness.

After collecting several fragments, she spotted what she knew was the rim of a whole shell partially buried in a small tidal pool. Uncovered, it was a magnificent, flawless creation of purple, rose, and pink.

But as she turned it in her hand, she discovered that it was occupied. Eileen suddenly found herself debating whether or not to take the shell back to the house. She weighed the pros—no one will miss it, most people don't like the slimy snail things that live inside, it's a perfect shell—and the cons— it is someone's home, I can't evict him, I'll feel guilty and won't enjoy the shell.

Finally, she put the shell back in the sand and walked on, surprised at her reaction to it.

Once home, however, she began to see the encounter as a threshold experience brought about by the conference. Previously, the oneness she felt with the world extended primarily to its more majestic aspects: the rivers, oceans, mountains, trees, and moon.

"My dilemma over the fate of the snail represented a new level of awareness for me. Ruminating on it, I realized that if I had been put to this test before the A.R.E. conference, I believe I would not have passed. But because time at Virginia Beach was so imbued by the themes of oneness, attunement, and connectedness to the creation, that magnificent shell was not to be my gift from the sea this year."

*   *   *

As more and more families came to Virginia Beach for the weeklong summer conferences, the need to occupy young people's hands and minds became apparent. In 1958, three teachers deeply involved in The Work set out to respond to that need. With Hugh Lynn's dynamic endorsement, the three researched the readings, marked off some space in the headquarters building amid the offices, and opened a two-week summer camp for youngsters.

One boy who attended the first camp session was John

LaPrelle. His mother, Mary, impressed with the positive impact that the time at A.R.E. had had on her son, offered a campsite on her farm at the edge of Jefferson National Forest in southwest Virginia.

The camp facilities slowly came into being, largely at the hands of volunteer carpenters.

Since the first days when the cabins opened to young people and later expanded to include adult and family sessions, there has been a magic about this rustic place in the woods where The Work is folded into the fabric of fields, ponds, hiking trails, and time set aside for meditation, prayer, and dream work.

That magic has made a lasting impression on many who have made the journey to "camp" and many look back on the experience as a defining time in their lives.

*   *   *

Glen's summers at camp, beginning when he was twelve years old, have helped shape his personal and professional life.

During his first session at camp, Glen learned that an injured fellow camper received treatments from a chiropractor. His curiosity led him to ask questions about the profession and the techniques used. Seeing a demonstration on a picnic table by the mess hall, he knew what he wanted to be.

Glen's six consecutive years at A.R.E. camp led him to read widely about Eastern philosophy, alternative medicine, and psychology. Working cooperatively with others in sports for the first time at camp, he took away from those summer weeks a commitment to work cooperatively to help others and an understanding of the responsibility that he had to take care of himself, as well.

He has continued to apply the principle he learned at camp in his professional life as a chiropractor, strengthening his relationship with his colleagues from China and adopting ideals and setting goals.

What he found as a youngster in the out-of-doors in southwest Virginia is an essence of what The Work is all about: cooperating and helping others.

* * *

Becky, at age sixteen, was in a typical teenage state: she was unhappy with herself, her friends, and what her young life seemed to be offering her. She was often depressed, her grades were falling, and she had little energy or social life. There were occasions when she'd try to shake off her attitude, but she'd eventually slip back into the same state.

Her mother, monitoring her daughter's behavior, felt the teenager needed a chance to get away from home, to face a new challenge or experience, and to start to view herself as an individual.

A.R.E. Camp seemed, to both Becky's mother and her stepdad, to be an answer; but they didn't push it on her. Once the teenager's questions were satisfactorily answered, she agreed to register for the camp's Next Step program.

There was something different in Becky's voice when she called home some weeks later. Despite a cut knee, Becky had joined a group of fellow campers for a week of backpacking on the Appalachian Trail. She reported that she'd endured hornet stings, swollen feet, and heavy rains. While she didn't report it, her mother sensed in her daughter's voice a real sense of pride and accomplishment.

In addition to her suitcase, backpack, and duffel bag, Becky brought home from camp a major change in herself. Her mother and stepdad could sense a new inner confidence, an ability to cooperate on an adult level, and a willingness to state her opinion and not feel slighted if a different choice was made.

When she returned from her days at A.R.E. camp, Becky, in her own words, felt "liked for herself"—not for what she had or who her brothers and parents were—just for being herself. What greater gift could be given to the young?

That gift, wrapped in the rustic setting of Virginia's mountains, is what A.R.E. Camp holds for all who arrive at the summer sessions. It is a place to introduce all who come to the Creator's handiwork in nature. Equally important, to introduce many of the campers, like Becky, to their true selves:

Then, the purposes, the import of the earthly sojourn of each soul is to meet self, to overcome those weaknesses in self, and become more and more adaptable to the spiritual truths that are a part of each and every entity. 1362-1

*   *   *

The letters from prisons throughout the country had been drifting into the A.R.E. irregularly and without a designated resting place.

Judith Stevens's job responsibilities in the early 1970s were in the A.R.E. Press and shipping department, but she saw an additional opportunity in the neglected letters. She began to answer them.

That effort, at first represented by a handful of letters tucked in a file folder, began to grow into cabinets full of correspondence between the prison population and those on the A.R.E. staff and in the volunteer ranks who wanted to share The Work with those behind bars.

The response was overwhelming and positive. Many of those in prison were rethinking their lives and their actions and wanted guidance. As word of The Work began to circulate within the prison populations, requests came for books and visitations. By 1974, nearly thirty Search for God Study Groups had been established in correctional facilities in twelve states.

The program became known as Over the Wall, but Judith Stevens led staff members and volunteers through the walls and the bars, meeting personally with prisoners and helping to start Study Groups and explain the meaning and the promise of The Work.

Today, more than 9,000 books are sent annually by the staff and volunteers of the A.R.E. prison program to prison libraries and individual inmates. The support from A.R.E. headquarters has encouraged inmate leaders to form groups, meeting in dayrooms and prison yards, to discuss the life-changing ideas in the information that came through Edgar Cayce.

The letters from inmates come unabated, some asking for more information and more books. Others, however, testify to the power of The Work in the lives of individuals who want to change and who are, with help, changing.

Chapter 11

FROM THE FILES: CAMP AND PRISON

Camp was a test of my beliefs. I went there with low self-esteem, yet knowing deep inside that I was okay and a worthwhile and interesting person. Camp brought out that faith and helped it come closer to the surface, because people accepted me for who I was and encouraged me to be that person without any hindrances. I came to believe in myself.

* * *

Most of all, camp life provided a positive role model of how to integrate the concepts from the readings (and other sources) into everyday life. It taught me how to interact with people in a constructive manner, how to keep the events in my life in perspective, and how to keep trying, every day, to be a better person . . . I can't even imagine what kind of life I would be leading today without the fundamentals that camp taught me.

* * *

Without a doubt, fellow A.R.E. campers are my spiritual family. Recalling the meditation grove to my inner eye can instantly bring back "the peace that passeth all understanding." Dreams of camp always bring the most significant spiritual messages. My experiences there are a measuring rod for all following paths. Applying in my relationships the profound yet simple truths learned at camp will continue to involve me the rest of my life.

*   *   *

I truly thank you for what you're doing for me while I'm incarcerated; maybe one day in the near future I will be able to help you in some way, God willing. For right now, all I can tell you is that I am truly thankful to you for all the help you have brought into my life. Thank you again and may God bless you at all times.

*   *   *

Having set the ideal of providing service to children, in tapping into the well of creative arts, I feel much more confident of a successful return to life outside of prison confinement . . . the books you have provided thus far have proven more beneficial than any other material matter ever introduced in this lifetime. Perceptions have been altered in ways where much that seemed beyond understanding is now crystal clear. Anger at insensitive indifference, manifested on a daily basis within prison settings, no longer burns white hot to the detriment of all concerned.

Am looking forward to hearing from you. Thanks so very much for the help you have been. May God bless you all.

*   *   *

A couple of months ago I wrote you a request for a copy of A Search for God *and along with that book you sent* Your Life: Why It Is the Way It Is and What You Can Do About It. *I would like to take this time to thank you for the material that I received from your association. It has given me great insight into the Creator, myself, and others.*

*   *   *

I am a forty-five-year-old black male. I am doing a two-year stint for petty theft. I don't consider myself a bad person. It's just sometimes, given the inconsistencies in my environment, I have a tendency to make my own laws. But as a consequence of my studies, I have realized that there are Universal Laws. I will allow them (the laws) to rehabilitate and transform me into the person that I want, need, and deserve to be . . .

So as I stated before, I will never finish reading the material that I have already received, but if at all possible could you forward me any books, newspapers, magazines, etc. Anything! Anything that will aid in my transforming process to the Higher Self. I have six months left to do, and I would like to spend it preparing and building a better life. It's already happening.

*   *   *

Thank you for the books. The materials on karma and re-incarnation in There Is a River *have been of invaluable help. What the penal system couldn't do in the past two years, this book did in two months. It gave me a proper perspective as to what was wrong with me. To love my enemy has been an insane concept. But Edgar Cayce's messages on karma and reincarnation allow me to perceive how practical and reasonable it is to love my enemy. Understanding this concept just a little bit has made my life in here less stressful, and I strive to understand more.*

I am hard-headed and ignorant, yet your programs were able to slowly open my mind to the truth. The experience I have had with your organization has been profound. Thank you for the experience, for your time, and for your energy. I am blessed to have crossed your path.

Chapter 12

THE TEMPLE BEAUTIFUL

The meeting would forever change the life of Edgar Cayce and, as a result, make better the lives of thousands in the years to come.

The twenty-three-year-old Cayce had lost his voice, following the onset of frequent headaches and a prescribed sedative that had rendered him dazed and disoriented. Several doctors had examined him and tried to remedy the condition to no avail. A hypnotist had tried to cure him, but Edgar had failed to yield to the post-suggestion.

Now a second hypnotist, Al Layne, was trying to help. His plan was to ask Edgar to talk about his own condition when Edgar reached the point at which he would no longer take the hypnotist's suggestion.

Edgar had discovered in his earlier sessions that it was his own thought that put him to sleep, no matter what the hypnotist said or did. Layne agreed to let the young Cayce do as much as he could.

Edgar lay down on the couch and put himself to sleep. Al Layne began to talk in a soft voice, requesting that Cayce view his own body and describe the trouble in his throat.

Edgar at first began to mumble. Then, clearing his throat, he began to speak in a normal voice and described the cause of his condition—a partial paralysis of the muscles of the vocal cord—and the remedy—increasing circulation to the affected area.

Layne gave the suggestion to increase the circulation, and, slowly, blood began to flow to Edgar's chest and throat, turning them a deep red.

After twenty minutes of self-prescribed treatment, Edgar was told by Layne to awaken; and when he did, his voice had returned to normal.

Despite his confusion and doubts about the extraordinary ability he had demonstrated, Edgar worked with Al Layne, who brought increasing numbers of cases to Edgar.

Only months after curing his own disorder, he was asked to help Aime Dietrich, a five-year-old girl who suffered frequent convulsions and whose mind had not developed since she contracted grippe at the age of two. Doctors and medical specialists had been unable to help her.

Edgar's initial reading for the child indicated that she had injured her back days before contracting the disease, and the grippe germs had settled in her spine, causing the problems. His reading recommended a series of osteopathic adjustments. Once the adjustments had been properly made, the child began to improve. Three months later, Layne reported to Edgar that the little girl had suffered no more convulsions and that her mental abilities were allowing her to catch up in schoolwork with children of her own age.

Edgar, as a young boy, had seen the vision of an angel as he sat in his private retreat in the woods, reading the Bible.

"Tell me what you would like most of all, so that I may give it to you," the vision said.

The boy replied, "Most of all I would like to be helpful to others, and especially to children when they are sick."

Aime Dietrich's recovery was but one early indication that Edgar Cayce's prayer had been answered. During his lifetime, he would give nearly 9,000 health readings for those who came to him for help. Those readings have become the foundation for clinics and institutes and the practices of individual physicians who transform lives by helping to heal the body, mind, and spirit.

Edgar Cayce's success at curing himself of his paralyzed

vocal cord muscles sidetracked a promising career as a photographer and began a lifetime of service known as The Work, which continues to heal others today.

*   *   *

Diana, at age thirty-five, was diagnosed with rheumatoid arthritis and within months was in constant pain and nearly helpless.

Her doctors prescribed numerous drugs, including a chemotherapy drug. At first she believed that the pills and shots would contain the disease and she would be able to manage her life. But each new drug failed to help, and Diana was confronted with having to live with the pain or face the prospect of more and more toxic drugs.

She had known about Edgar Cayce since her late teens but hadn't been close to The Work for some time. After two years of fighting a losing battle against her disease, she began to think about Cayce's health readings.

She joined the A.R.E. and requested information in the readings on rheumatoid arthritis. Her friends and her pharmacist were skeptical when she began a search for some of the oils recommended in the readings. Her doctors cautioned her against trying holistic remedies, but at the same time they also confessed that their profession didn't know the cause or the cure for her condition.

Diana stopped the chemotherapy drug and began to follow the Cayce regimen of Atomidine therapy, Epsom salt baths, and a recommended diet. After two months she knew that she was improving.

A recurrence of the condition, however, made her think more deeply about the Cayce material and the possible cause of the disease. Medical journals stated that her arthritis might be a psychosomatic disease caused by stress. Reading more of the Cayce information, she began to understand that the cause might be her reaction—negative emotions—to the stress, not the stress itself.

She began to think back to events in her life that occurred just before she became ill. One was the terrible death of her brother-in-law, a deputy sheriff, at the hands of a violent husband who was threatening his wife and children. The other was the death of her beloved golden Labrador, killed by her neighbor's dogs. Her neighbor had refused to acknowledge that the dogs had been responsible, despite obvious evidence.

Diana acknowledged that she felt a hatred toward those who had inflicted tragedy into her life. She realized that as her attitude worsened, so did the arthritis. Reflecting on the readings—"Mind is the builder"—she began to forgive those whom she held in contempt.

"The Cayce material," she said, "has been a true Godsend in helping me understand what has been happening in my life and in giving me ways to hope and to heal."

*   *   *

George's condition had been diagnosed as an infected kidney after he entered the hospital complaining of back pain.

It was only when he called his wife on the planned day of his release that the true difficulty came to light. His conversation with her was strange and unintelligible; he had confused many of his words while speaking to her. He remained in the hospital and a specialist was summoned. George was unable to recall the names of several commonplace objects that the doctor asked him to name, and he was unable to correctly write down the name of one of the United States.

The doctor diagnosed George as having a condition called bacterial endocarditis, an infection of the heart lining. Apparently an embolus had moved from the heart lining through the blood stream and had damaged the kidney and the brain, affecting the area controlling verbalization. He was suffering from aphasia.

Awaiting transfer to a major hospital the next day, George was unable to lie down because of a severe headache. He sat up all night, his back against the wall at the head of the bed and his feet crossed underneath him.

Although he had read nearly every book about Cayce and The Work published during the previous decade, George didn't know very much—on a conscious level—about meditation and affirmations, and he hadn't said a prayer in many years.

That night, however, he repeated to himself over and over, "I must recover. I must recover." He thought of his wife and three children and his work as a teacher, writer, lecturer, and theater director, all of which required the use of words.

As he repeated the words "I must recover," he also sent energy to the affected area on the left side of his head. He began to actually feel something physical happening inside his brain, as though mental waves were affecting the embolism and the damaged tissue.

After his transfer to the university hospital the next morning, he was put on antibiotics to kill the bacteria. There was no known treatment to reverse the brain damage he had already suffered. But without explanation, the aphasia began to clear up, and within a few days all effects of it had disappeared. George remained in the hospital for five weeks to insure that the bacterial infection was gone.

Although there is no proof that the affirmations and the mental efforts that George expended that night cured his condition, he remains positive that they did.

"I now feel that night—because of the critical need I felt—I opened a healing channel to my higher self, which then restructured the damaged cells of my brain . . .

"By that point in my life, I had read enough of the Cayce material to know that all of the outer life is a symbolic manifestation of the inner life, and that I had five weeks to ponder my heart condition and the fact that I was not very loving at that time. I now also believe that illness was a message to me—which I was able to correctly interpret, since I had studied the Cayce material—to become more loving."

*   *   *

Tim, eighteen years old and a short time in the Navy, was diagnosed with neurofibromatosis. The disease causes cafe-au-lait marks on the skin and benign skin tumors. Tim's type of NF had also affected the bones in his legs.

The diagnosis was devastating to Tim and to his mother. Although conventional medicine held no real hope for his condition, his mother turned to the Cayce material. She had Tim's name placed on numerous prayer lists. She began researching the readings, and, as a result, Tim began to take a daily dose of Calcios, a syrupy paste of free calcium that was recommended scores of times in the readings.

When doctors operated on Tim's left leg, they were confronted with a major medical challenge. They performed such extensive reconstructive work on the bone that Tim was still in a brace a year later. He needed nearly a gallon of blood during the operation, and doctors performed two major grafts.

By the time the operation on his right leg was performed, Tim had been taking the Calcios for a while and had been the subject of prayers through A.R.E. healing groups. In this operation, he required far less surgery, no blood transfusions, and no grafts.

His mother reported, "Both legs looked identical in the X rays . . . but the second leg had started to heal on its own after we started our program . . . in addition, the first leg is in a process of accelerated healing . . . since he started using the Calcios. Since Tim has been on the various prayer lists . . . all external, visible growths have disappeared— soon after they started growing. There have been no recorded instances of spontaneous healing of internal growths or of external growths disappearing. Tim is the only case that either National Institute of Health or the N.F. Clinic has ever seen."

Two more lives, that of a mother and her son, were changed forever because a mother put faith and trust in suggestions found in The Work.

* * *

Bill McGarey, even as a medical student, wondered why medical schools didn't teach courses in healing. He had become familiar with unusual therapies early on and believed that such remedies could be beneficial.

When he and his wife, Gladys, also a physician, began practicing in his hometown of Wellsville, Ohio, in 1948, his interest in alternative treatments quickly brought him words of caution from fellow doctors. An unexpected detour into the United States Air Force as a flight surgeon from 1953 to 1955 gave him time to think about his future. When he was discharged, he decided he wouldn't return to his hometown because of the confining attitudes about medicine. Deep down, he heard God say, "Bill McGarey, I've got something for you to do."

He and Gladys moved their practice to Phoenix, Arizona, and Bill became more and more interested in metaphysical and spiritual paths. In 1956, the two doctors met Hugh Lynn Cayce and joined the A.R.E. As they became familiar with the readings, they began to cautiously use some of the spiritual-mental suggestions in their practice.

Hugh Lynn constantly urged the two to work with the physical readings, and the McGareys moved slowly and carefully in that direction. They visited Virginia Beach to research the readings and to lecture on concepts in The Work that related to health.

Finally, in 1970, they decided to convert their conventional family practice to one using the therapeutic techniques in the readings. The A.R.E. Clinic came into being as a separate nonprofit corporation.

Eight years later, the clinic began a residential treatment program called the Temple Beautiful Program, after the program outlined in the readings during the period of Ra-Ta in Ancient Egypt:

> In the Temple Beautiful there were the expressions of the service as an activity to maintain and to purify

the bodies for the necessary associations of spiritual understandings in material bodies. 281-025

Working with health information in the readings, the McGareys' ideal was to treat patients and do research at the clinical level with the Cayce concepts of healing and to teach those concepts to other health-care personnel and to the public. Along the way, individuals have been changed as well as healed of physical ailments.

* * *

One of the patients in the Temple Beautiful Program was a woman in her eighties. Her condition was not severe, but she had some trouble walking, her memory was at times poor, and she was unable to sleep well.

As she became involved in the program, it became apparent that she was highly critical—critical of herself as a person and as a painter and critical of others.

In addition to the medical treatments, she received the gentleness, the consideration, and the understanding—the unconditional love—that the readings suggest all of us should give and receive.

In less than two weeks, she had undergone dramatic changes. She was sleeping well. Her memory was better, and she was a joy to be with. She began to recall insightful dreams, and her physical condition overall was greatly improved.

Before she left the clinic, she insisted on hugging everyone, an act that would have shocked her at the outset of the program. A card she sent after she returned home expressed her "deepest gratitude and admiration." She wrote, "I have never seen so much talent and devotion before."

* * *

David, a lawyer with a pregnant wife and a son, was twenty-seven when he was told that he had Hodgkin's disease. His life turned upside down.

For six months he received radiation treatments, and he found himself living with the day-to-day fear that the disease would return.

It was during this time of silent fear that he heard an inner voice that told him he had to know that he was cured— Not hope, not think, not believe, but *know* that the disease was gone.

He was not knowledgeable about the complex makeup and interrelationship of body, mind, and spirit, but he began to educate himself. To strengthen his growing belief that he could know that he was cured, he began reading inspirational literature. One of the books was *The Sleeping Prophet.*

Continuing chemotherapy and radiation, he also contacted the A.R.E. for the files on Hodgkin's disease. At first he was disappointed because he could not understand the language in the readings and because the suggested treatments varied from case to case. Nonetheless, he persevered and decided to adopt from the files a plan that he could follow for himself. One reading in particular seemed understandable to him and he made up his mind to follow the recommendations, as best he could:

First, let's give that as may aid in relieving the tensions:

One hour each day for three days in succession, apply the hot Castor Oil Packs across the abdominal area and entirely *around* the body—that is, over the abdominal area as well as over the back area. Apply these as warm as the body can well stand. This may give a little distress at the first period. Afterward there will be much ease.

After taking the third Pack, on the evening of the third day, you see, take internally three tablespoonsful of Pure Olive Oil.

After resting a day following the series of the Castor Oil Packs, begin then with osteopathic adjustments; with special reference to the coccyx centers and the

6th and 7th dorsal center. Do not attempt to make *all* adjustments necessary at one time, but have a series of treatments to gradually make adjustment.

In ten days or two weeks, repeat the three-day series of the Castor Oil Packs, one hour each day, followed by the Olive Oil internally. Continue with these at such intervals until there has been the adjusting of the pressures in the coccyx and the upper dorsal areas, and until the rest of the cerebrospinal system is coordinated.

Systematically we would have a cleansing of the colon with the hydrotherapy. Do be careful in the administration of these colonics. Have *two* such colonics in ten days, and then continue these systematically—at regular intervals—until there is no indication of the mucous that will be the natural accumulation from the system by the application of the Oil Packs. But have two during the first ten day period, you see, and then farther apart, as felt necessary by the one administering same. 2643-1

After studying all of the readings, David decided to use the castor oil packs, osteopathic adjustments, and an ingestion of Atomidine solution.

Although his wife wasn't familiar with Edgar Cayce, she was a willing helpmate for her husband, often preparing the castor oil packs and arranging the bed to prevent the oil from leaking onto the mattress.

On occasion when he was using the packs, he would meditate or read, always keeping in mind that the readings stressed that attitude was the most important ingredient in healing.

Dr. John Pike was the only osteopath in David's area. Initially embarrassed to tell the physician that he was following advice from Edgar Cayce, David found himself in the care of a doctor who, many years earlier, had been recommended to another patient by Cayce, although the two had never met.

David saw Dr. Pike for three years, following guidance from the readings about the frequency of treatments.

Now becoming comfortable with the information in the readings, David wrote to Dr. William McGarey at the A.R.E. Clinic to better understand the properties of Atomidine. The readings recommended the liquid for a wide range of illnesses but warned that too much, because of its iodine content, might be unwise if the patient was getting iodine from other sources. Dr. McGarey responded quickly and also suggested use of the wet cell and fumes from apple brandy placed in a charred oaken keg. David added these to his treatments.

Three years after David discovered The Work, he ceased his regular pattern of treatments. They had, he felt, served their purpose. Two years later, his doctors pronounced their findings: they considered him cured.

The man who had stumbled onto The Work in an effort to free himself from a dreaded disease found help and change in the treatments and the philosophy in the readings. He summed up his view of the cause for his cure by citing a reading:

> Let those that minister know that all healing, all force and all power comes from the Infinite; that those influences and powers that work in and through them, in making the application, can, will, through those promises He has given, manifest health, strength, vitality, for this body. 735-4

* * *

John, simply put, had a bad attitude. He naturally rebelled at any rules or regulations that required things to be done in a certain way. Compounding his poor outlook, he was able to easily sink into depression whenever something went wrong, looking to see who could be blamed.

Physically, John's stomach was a barometer of his emotions. When he became frustrated or depressed, his stomach let him know, grumbling and churning.

He was leading a life that was tempting trouble, and when it came, it arrived in a major way. He had begun to notice some bleeding at one point but paid little attention to it. During a tennis match—a passion of his—he mentioned the bleeding to his playing partner, a physician friend. The doctor suggested an exam. The examination showed cancer, and surgeons removed fifteen inches of his colon.

During his ten-day stay in the hospital, John began to think about his situation. He concluded that he had laid the groundwork for the disease to invade his body with his negative attitude, with his penchant for constant activity, and his easy slide into a depressed state when things didn't go well.

He began to realize that he hadn't taken time to truly enjoy life and that he'd taken his strong body and near-perfect health for granted. Now, at age sixty-two, he found himself no longer in control of his life.

Several days after his surgery, an oncologist walked into John's hospital room and told him the news that he had only a short time to live but that chemotherapy would help to prolong his life. He explained that without chemotherapy, the cancer would spread to the liver, sapping what was left of John's energy and becoming terminal. Chemotherapy, the doctor told John, was "an absolute must."

It was another blow. A further discussion with the oncologist, while John's wife was present, painted a dire picture of the future: intravenous injection of chemicals directly into the liver for five consecutive days, to be repeated eight times every six weeks for the next forty-eight weeks. The doctor's last admonition was that John didn't have much time to weigh the decision, that the therapy should start within three weeks of the surgery to be most effective. John and his wife told the doctor that they would make a decision after he returned home.

Sitting in his den after his return home and waiting for his wife to return from a shopping trip, John noticed a brochure from the A.R.E. Clinic on the coffee table. He remembered that his wife had said the clinic was a holistic center where treatment was directed at the mind, the body, and the spirit. He picked up the phone and called.

When he ended his conversation with Dr. McGarey, John felt relieved, knowing that there was an alternative to chemotherapy. When his wife returned home, she agreed, and John secured a place in the clinic's Temple Beautiful Program.

John and his wife arrived in Phoenix on a Thursday afternoon. By Friday morning, John was taking his first steps on a path of balancing body, mind, and spirit. It was a new path for him, but a path well-traveled by those who knew about Edgar Cayce and The Work.

"I think that most of my life I've only been cognizant of my mind, taken my body for granted, and fed my spirit a near-starvation diet," John remembers thinking during his time at the clinic. That was about to change dramatically.

Sharing life stories with others in the program, relating dreams and having them interpreted, getting massages, colonics, and biofeedback, learning to recognize auras, and experiencing music and dance therapy opened John to the possibilities of a different and greatly enriched life.

When John returned home, he brought a new attitude with him. Meditation, which he had made no time for in earlier years, became part of each day.

At his office when he would react to problems with his old approach of looking for someone to blame, he was able to catch himself and shift his focus to harmony in his business dealings rather than simply the bottom line.

He began to pay close attention to his physical well being, removing the self-imposed pressure to get things done at once and acknowledging that when he felt tired, he needed to back away from work. He modified his diet, in keeping with suggestions he had received at the clinic. He returned to the tennis court, to hiking, to trips with his wife, and to living the way that he wanted to and "feeling good doing so."

John's six-month checkup showed normal results for the blood tests and the colonoscopy.

What they didn't show was the change in John's attitude and the change in his life.

*   *   *

The diagnosis of prostatic cancer was the beginning of a journey from confusion and disease to the light, Charles recalled. Initially stunned at the doctor's words, Charles collected himself and told the doctor to schedule surgery.

Two days later, Charles awoke from the surgery and learned that the doctor had removed about two pounds of flesh, including the lymph nodes in the area of the prostate. All had gone well, the doctor reported, and daily radiation for the next six weeks was prescribed.

Following the treatments, Charles regained his feeling of good health and returned to a normal life, believing that he had conquered the disease.

Years passed with no medical problems, but Charles's life took a downward turn. He found himself mired in misery and unhappiness. The continuing love and support of his wife was his only solace.

Then the cancer returned. A routine blood test detected it, and a biopsy confirmed the disease. The physician recommended removal of the prostate and the bladder. Charles faced a future with a urine bag attached to his side. Active and a committed golfer, the image was a grim prospect. He and his wife cried together for a moment.

Then something magnificent happened to him. In a second it seemed to him that a Force—a loving, irresistible Force—took command of his life. He turned to his wife and told her that he didn't want to live like that, being someone else's responsibility. He said "No" to the surgery, and they left the hospital.

In a serene silence they drove home, knowing that a new life was about to begin.

Charles and his wife had been members of the A.R.E. for years and regarded Edgar Cayce as a figure of integrity and healing. At home, Charles's wife remembered an article in the A.R.E. magazine about a man who had been healed at a holistic center in Phoenix. They dug through past issues of the magazine until they found the article. Charles called the A.R.E. Clinic and arranged to enter the Temple Beautiful Program.

As if to test his resolve, Charles started to bleed only days before his scheduled trip to the clinic. He reentered the hospital, and the bleeding continued off and on for two days. His doctor told him not to ride in a car; in view of his problem, it would be dangerous. Faced with a plane trip to Phoenix, Charles began to have doubts about his ability to get there; he confided in his wife that he didn't think he was going to make it.

But the bleeding stopped, and the two were soon on a flight from New York to Phoenix, gaining confidence as they neared the clinic.

Charles's assessment of what happened to him goes to the heart of what The Work offers about the interconnectedness of body, mind, and spirit:

"I know that the reason I got cancer the first time was because I had been living in such a way that internal heat and confusion had become my habitual climate. I would do anything to get ahead. I was materially oriented, thinking about success. I was aggressive, thinking about how much money I could make, and I wasn't particularly adverse to hurting the feelings of others if it was necessary to promote my future.

"I had created a condition of moral internal combustion which affected my health and mental outlook. It had to find an outlet somewhere, and it found it, causing my cancer. It was hell. Cancer had come to me to compel me to change."

Charles quickly found that he was a large and active part of his own healing process at the clinic. Exercises, a multitude of therapies, and a new diet became part of his daily activities. He and his wife came home with commitments to a different way of life including periods of daily meditation and a changed diet.

"The two human beings who carried me in those years

were Carl Jung and Edgar Cayce. They became my bench-marks, and I read everything I could get of theirs for five years. I consider Cayce among the ten greatest Americans of all time. Jung and Cayce were the two who kept me going until I got to the A.R.E. Clinic. It is my profound conviction that an acceptance and understanding of the life divine is what breathes life into every treatment I experienced at the Clinic," he wrote of his experience.

"Being clever and right no longer interested me. I wanted life and serenity. All I had to do was change."

With the help of clinic personnel, his own determination, and a strong belief in Cayce's work, Charles did change.

*   *   *

Word of the health readings spread throughout the medical profession. Other doctors joined the McGareys in applying information in The Work to individuals who needed help. John Pagano, a doctor of chiropractic, became interested in the Cayce work during his college years. He focused particularly on what the readings had to say about the benefits of spinal adjustments. As he delved more and more deeply into The Work, he began to understand the importance that the readings attributed to proper diet. He has become an internationally recognized leader in the cure of psoriasis, using the guidance in the readings as a foundation for his healing.

Through his skilled hands, individuals who had given up hope of finding a cure for the scourge of psoriasis have been cured:

*   An eight-year-old girl, who had developed psoriasis at age six, came to him. Her condition had worsened during conventional treatment. Dr. Pagano's chiropractic treatments and a change in diet cleared her of all lesions in six months. Years later she remained free of the disease.

*   A thirty-four-year-old woman suffered with the disease for twenty-two years and had tried nearly every avail-

able therapeutic measure without success. Within three months of being under Dr. Pagano's care, she had improved. Two years later, still following his diet recommendations, she was dramatically better.

• A thirty-six-year-old man, suffering for two years, found no help with dermatologists and normal treatments. Dr. Pagano put him on a diet—he was extremely overweight—and within twelve months he had lost sixty pounds and the disease had gone.

There are a multitude of similar cases in Dr. Pagano's files. They represent more than records of a successful medical treatment. Each individual had come out of desperation, seeking relief from a disease that saps self-esteem and a positive attitude about life, in addition to the physical discomfort.

Once healed, they left with gratitude certainly, but, more important, with a new and a changed outlook on their life.

*   *   *

Harold Reilly, a well-known and respected physiotherapist in Manhattan, became an instrument for transformation through the readings. Similar to Dr. John Pike's experience, Reilly had never heard of Edgar Cayce when individuals began to come to him for treatment, saying, "I had a reading from Edgar Cayce and I was told to see you." Reilly would review the typed copies of the readings and follow the suggestions, finding them effective. He and Cayce finally met and became close friends. Their friendship became the cornerstone of the Cayce/Reilly School of Massotherapy, which has changed the lives of those who come as students and those who come to seek better health.

*   *   *

The young Japanese woman and her son left New York and headed to Virginia Beach. Behind her was a vagabond life of sorts. She had left her job with a Japanese trading company, had moved to San Francisco to become an accomplished jazz singer, had married and divorced, and moved to New York.

It was while Asato was in New York that she realized that she might have a gift. She had studied shiatsu, a Japanese pressure point therapy. While combating a kidney problem, she massaged the kidney reflect point in her foot. She realized that she had been able to heal herself and she began to think that she might have healing in her hands.

She enrolled in the massotherapy school, and she began to study the readings, particularly the *Search for God* chapter on "Know Thyself."

After graduation, she offered clients her carefully constructed "Transformative Meditation Healing Therapy," knowing that she could help her clients open to spiritual change. She took as her guidance the words from the Cayce readings, "Spirit is the life, mind is the builder, the physical is the result."

Janice, one of her clients, was changed as the result of Asato's treatments.

"From the moment Asato touched me, I felt a sense of total trust. I felt she was working with my vibrational field. I believe that at a certain point in her treatment, there is a window of opportunity within the spirit or the soul to receive the universal life force. I think she serves as a mediator to bringing in this positive energy.

"Since Asato's treatments, my own work has changed. After my first session with her, clients began to tell me that my energy felt different. I can also feel their energy more acutely."

Janice's past was laced with unhappy moments as she struggled to know who she was. A workshop brochure, received because she was an A.R.E. member, started to provide answers to her question, and the treatments she received from Asato spurred her on.

The result, she says, "is the happiness I have today, just by finding out who I truly am."

Touched by The Work, people like Asato and Janice expand farther and farther the ability of the Cayce material to change lives.

* * *

Other efforts have begun to expand the reach of the transformative powers triggered by the Cayce material. The medical profession, once cynical about alternative treatments, has opened its collective mind to the benefits of the body-mind-spirit connection. To assist in demonstrating the health benefits of The Work, a research institute is now working with individuals who suffer a variety of disorders addressed by the readings. Under the auspices of the Meridian Institute, health-care professionals and others intimately familiar with the Cayce material are making a lasting impact on the lives of those who come to them.

* * *

Jan was diagnosed with Parkinson's disease at age forty-nine.

A psychotherapist who led an active life of service, she found herself increasingly sapped of energy. Prescribed medication helped for a time, but three years of combating the disease finally left her with little more than the ability to dress herself and prepare a meal before she needed to rest for an hour or more. Her career, which she had worked so hard to establish and which gave her great satisfaction, had been reduced to a couple of clients a day.

Jan finally reached the point where she had to give up her practice. The disease had taken her livelihood and reduced her life to that of a recluse, who rarely left home because she was unable to drive.

She found, however, that she was willing to try nearly any possible solution. She began working with a number of alternative methods, including Reiki, hypnosis, psychic readings, and psychic healers. A close friend, who was a

member of the A.R.E., encouraged her to try Cayce's approach
to Parkinson's. She ordered the wet cell described in the
readings and began her own treatment program. Shortly
after that, she was contacted by the Meridian Institute,
which had established a research project on Parkinson's.

Jan soon found herself, along with more than a dozen
others, immersed in a Cayce-based program. Diets outlined in the readings, wet cell applications, prayer from the
Glad Helpers, meditation, chiropractic adjustments,
dream work, an introspective focus on attitudes and emotions, and the setting of ideals made up her week.

When Jan returned home, she summoned friends to help
her continue the protocols that had been taught by the
Meridian staff. After working with the program at home for
five months, Jan had regained enough coordination to be
able to drive a car again. Although unable at that time to
return to her practice, she reported: "I feel a pervading
sense of inner peace and strength, knowing that God's
presence is a given in my life."

Others who participated in the Meridian program found
positive change after they returned home. They shared
their newfound attitudes:

One wrote, "My health and happiness grow stronger
each day. I can tell even after this short time that good
changes are happening in my body. The Wet Cell works. My
smile has returned and I'm sharing it with my friends. I am
no longer such a 'dead pan.' I have more stamina . . . I am
more aware that the Lord walks with me."

Another reported, "I have moved even more clearly into
absolute certainty that healing is taking place or will take
place. I have the sense, actually, that this is the final chapter in my seven-year quest for this healing . . . "

Jan herself reported, "I have come alive again and, bit by
bit, am regaining strength, stamina, and coordination. I felt
God's hand placed upon me in blessing to be able to be part
of this experience."

Chapter 13

FROM THE FILES: THE HEALTH READINGS

I am no longer under medical treatment for arthritis or prinzmetals angina. I attribute both breakthroughs to daily meditation and a change in attitudes.

I was filled with anger, hate, and self-pity when I came to the Cayce material. Study Group work convinced me that love and forgiveness was a better way and I have benefited in all areas of my life.

I am closer to God now than I ever was before. I feel the strength and love of the Creative Forces whenever I take time to ask. In addition, I find more and more that personal guidance is mine for the asking. And more and more, I think to ask.

For the first time in my life, I am now at peace (most of the time) with the world around me. I am more patient, more loving, more forgiving. The readings of Edgar Cayce and the help from the Study Group in applying the lessons to my daily life has brought me improved health, joy, and love.

* * *

A friend introduced me to Edgar Cayce about twelve or thirteen years ago, when I was struggling to overcome drug addiction. I was unable to grasp spirituality from the 12-step programs, though they were a great help to me in other ways.

Reading the Search for God *series and actually under-standing spirituality from Edgar Cayce's perspective and concepts was truly a blessed gift of grace. I began to apply the spiritual concepts in my life and relations with others, and I can now report that, by the grace of God, I have not used drugs or alcohol for nine years and eight months.*

*   *   *

My physical health has improved vastly due to better diet, exercise, positive attitude, prayer, and determination not to give up.

I don't just believe, but now I live by the precept that "with God, all things are possible." What a long way I have come in the past twelve to thirteen years and a lot of thanks go to Edgar Cayce and the A.R.E.

In every way I could possibly conceive, my life on this planet has changed for the better through my association (and learning) with the A.R.E.

*   *   *

I used to take twenty-seven pills every day—now I only take two pills a week. I used to weigh 220 pounds—now I weigh 165. I used to have bad allergies—I am rarely sick now.

My attitude about life has improved one hundred percent. I always felt like I didn't belong in this life. Edgar Cayce and the Lord have given me back my family and my life.

*   *   *

I had been an alcoholic for twelve years, when my sister-in-law gave me a book on Edgar Cayce. Though I was raised up in the Southern Baptist traditions, with an inquiring mind and with questions for which there seemed to be no answers, while reading about this man Cayce and his infor-mation, my mind suddenly opened and now I had the an-

swers I so long sought. Especially that one about the body being the temple of the living God.

I became aware that I was on my knees and weeping there in my living room. I stood up and then realized beyond a shadow of a doubt that I was no longer an alcoholic.

Thank you, Edgar Cayce, for caring enough to be of service to your fellow souls by being a channel of our Loving God and Savior.

*   *   *

I was very ill after stomach surgery and couldn't keep anything in my system. I was also told that I had pancreatic cancer. After using caster oil packs, my system improved and my pancreas healed. My whole attitude toward life has changed from limitation to the beginning of abundance. Emotions are now under control through the use of universal laws. By studying the readings I have found out why my life was the way it was. I will always thank God for the day I came to your library looking for one book.

*   *   *

There have been so many changes in my life since I came in contact with the Cayce material. My health, eating habits; I don't see people anymore, I see brothers and sisters. I pray daily for the world and thank God for Mr. Cayce. I wish everyone could know of this.

Chapter 14

A Personal Note

In December 1984 I found myself in a small office on the third floor of the A.R.E. headquarters building. I was mildly surprised at myself. Some of my family and a lot of my friends were shocked.

I was looking for a more reliable income than two years of freelance writing had contributed to my bank account. *Venture Inward* editor Robert Smith, a former newspaper colleague, had called me, looking for likely candidates to fill the job of managing editor for the magazine. I had given him a couple of names, listened and reciprocated during an exchange of news on our respective career paths since leaving newspapering, and put the phone back on the receiver. The more I thought about his requirements for the position and the more I thought about my desire to return to full-time work, the more I was tempted to call him back. Finally I picked the phone back up and called him, asking him to put my name in the hat of candidates if he felt I could help.

That phone call changed my life.

I didn't know much about Cayce and the A.R.E. My younger sister had read about him in her teens and had spent occasional time with several of her friends in the library, but she and I rarely talked of such subjects. I'd known Gladys Davis Turner through her nephew Teejay, when he and I were in our early teens and used to pal around with the same group of schoolmates, but I'd never inquired about Mr. Cayce. I had a vague respect for the organization, in part because some of my North-End Virginia Beach neighbors thought the organization was comprised of devil-worshippers. I knew enough to know that wasn't true, and I was impressed that the organization went about its business in a quiet, dignified way.

I confessed my lack of Cayce knowledge to Charles Thomas Cayce during my interview. He assured me that I'd quickly learn about the man and The Work, and he added that I'd make my own decision about whether or not I was comfortable on staff.

Behind me were twenty-seven years as an idealistic newspaper journalist. I had started down that path at age twenty, when I left college to work with my father on a weekly newspaper he'd started to crusade against local political corruption. Five years later, he'd mostly succeeded in shutting down the illegal activities that had invaded Virginia Beach, he and I had been featured in *Newsweek* magazine for courage in journalism, and he'd traded in his newspaper business to become caretaker for his dying wife, my mother.

I was left jobless with an incomplete college education, but with a lifelong belief that each person has an obligation to make a small part of the world a better place.

Ascendancy up the daily newspaper ladder to become one of the nation's youngest managing editors of a major daily newspaper, a flirtatious overture by *Time* magazine for me to join their staff, a stint as publisher-editor of a statewide magazine, authorship of four books, and a couple of years as editor of regional books had left me disillusioned about journalism and, in many ways, about people. I was drifting, without direction and without goals.

Thus I began work as managing editor of *Venture Inward*—knowing a great deal about my work, but very little about The Work.

Before the first week had ended, I, a wayward Episcopalian still trying to cope with the present, was plunged backward into my first past-life experience. The attendees of the annual A.R.E. Christmas party, held that year in the Conference Center, gathered in groups of staff and volunteers beneath banners of their respective astrological signs. A fellow Piscean—an older, attractive, very mannered lady—introduced herself and we chatted for a while. As she prepared to turn her attention elsewhere, she looked me in the eye and said, "I'm sure we knew each other in the time of Christ." I was dumbfounded, but polite enough to say, "You may well be right." It was a startling first lesson about concepts that are the foundation of The Work.

I had a patient and understanding mentor in Bob Smith. He had been attracted to the Cayce material years before he arrived in Virginia Beach to become an editorial writer for *The Virginian-Pilot* and subsequently the founding editor of *Venture Inward*. He guided me in my journey to learn about the organization's activities and its mission to others, and he answered a lot of questions about The Work and what it had meant and could mean to people. Often, I think he could sense what I needed or wanted to know, his answers coming before my questions were asked. Mostly I began to understand the power of The Work in a person's life by his example. He was calm, even in the midst of occasional pressures and crises that come with establishing a magazine. But more impressive, he was considerate, encouraging, at times even compassionate, towards everyone with whom he dealt.

As I learned from him, I also learned from others, both staff and members who came to visit. There was a genuine caring for others, for their progress and their problems, for each other as individuals. I began to understand, in my own mind, that this truly was love, a love born of the realization that we are indeed all one, inexorably connected by and with the Universal Force that creates everything. I had traveled a long way from the cynicism and the vaulting ambition that were a part of previous endeavors.

I also began traveling away from some destructive habits that I'd been living with. I took an honest look at myself and, for the first time, saw flaws. Old habits die hard, the saying goes, but they can be put to rest. The more I studied myself and the more I studied those around me as examples to emulate, the harder I worked at change. It wasn't easy at first, but it's become a satisfying challenge today.

I've carried a goal—some would call it an ideal—for a number of years. It was shortly after an interview that I did with Robert Adriance for *Venture Inward* that I adopted a blueprint as my own. I was trying to pry out of him some of the efforts he'd made through the years to keep The Work alive and reach out to others. At one point he mentioned the plaque over the doorway to the Library/Conference Center. It reads: "to make manifest the love of God and man."

An idealism too long in mothballs was again a part of my wardrobe.

I'm not presumptuous enough to think I'll achieve such a perfect state, but I am certain that I am the better, that my relationships are the better, and that, from time to time, others are the better for my striving.

Not too many years ago I was privileged to edit the manuscript which became the book *Your Life: Why It Is the Way It Is and What You Can Do About It*, by the late Bruce McArthur. Bruce and I, mostly by long-distance phone calls and lots of letters, became, I like to think, good friends as we shaped that manuscript. And he, whether he knew it or not, became another gracious mentor in my journey.

Even in its earliest draft, Bruce's writing and his knowledge of the universal laws and The Work spoke to me—mind, heart, and soul. As much perhaps to celebrate my own transformation as to pay deserved tribute to a special person, I wrote him on March 12, 1992:

> *This letter contains two reactions to your manuscript.*
> *One reaction is very personal. Under normal circumstances, such a reaction would have no proper place in*

a letter from an editor to a writer. Under any circum-
stances, my personal reaction to your work can have
no bearing on the final decisions that the A.R.E. Press
makes about [your book]. I am compelled, nonetheless,
to convey to you a sense of what your work means to
me.

There have been times in the past weeks, as I re-
viewed the manuscript, that I experienced the excite-
ment that comes with discovery. There has been, too, a
feeling of joy, a joy that has come with my increasing
comfort with who I am and where I am in this life and,
most importantly, where I can go—if I but continue to
work with myself and my relationship with God . . .

I am part of the unending parade of people who, by
whatever means, have been introduced to the Edgar Cayce
material. I, too, have been changed by The Work.

J.D.

EPILOGUE

The world is at the doorway to a new era, and the age-old questions and the age-old challenges remain. The Work goes forward in new and modern ways with renewed vigor and commitment. Its purpose is to help find answers to those questions and to help in meeting the challenges. Individuals now learn of Edgar Cayce and The Work through the channels of movies, television, and the Internet.

The Association for Research and Enlightenment is establishing new ways to assist individuals in applying the guidance in The Work. A health and rejuvenation center is taking form, and institutes are being structured to help people find their true purpose in life and to grasp the potential of their innate intuitive gifts. Every new endeavor is built upon the goal of facilitating personal growth and transformation—and ultimately global transformation—towards God using the legacy left by Edgar Cayce in over 14,000 readings.

That goal is as certain to be reached in future years as it has been in the past. The impact of The Work—past, present, and future—is in the testimony of those, like this person from a small town in Arkansas, who have discovered it and have applied it:

I have felt changes in every aspect of my life as a re-

sult of twenty years of study and attempts at application of the concepts in the readings. I can only hope that others have witnessed them.

The work is the most precious thing in life to me— right up there along with my family. We thank God for this knowledge every day of our lives.

The world needs it so desperately.

———————

You Can Receive Books Like This One and Much, Much More

You can begin to receive books in the *A.R.E. Membership Series* and many more benefits by joining the nonprofit Association for Research and Enlightenment, Inc., as a Sponsoring or Life member.

The A.R.E. has a worldwide membership that receives a wide variety of study aids, all aimed at assisting individuals in their spiritual, mental, and physical growth.

Every member of A.R.E. receives a copy of *Venture Inward*, the organization's bimonthly magazine; a periodic in-depth journal, *The New Millennium;* opportunity to borrow, through the mail, from a collection of more than 500 files on medical and metaphysical subjects; access to one of the world's most complete libraries on metaphysical and spiritual subjects; and opportunities to participate in conferences, international tours, a retreat-camp for children and adults, and numerous nationwide volunteer activities.

In addition to the foregoing benefits, Sponsoring and Life members also receive as gifts three books each year in the *A.R.E. Membership Series.*

If you are interested in finding out more about membership in A.R.E. and the many benefits that can assist you on your path to fulfillment, you can easily contact the Membership Department by writing Membership, A.R.E., 215 67th Street, Virginia Beach, VA 23451-2061 or by calling **1-800-333-4499** or faxing **1-757-422-6921.**

**Explore our electronic visitor's center on the Internet:
http://www.are-cayce.com**